RURAL EXODUS & SQUATTER SETTLEMENTS IN THE THIRD WORLD

Case of Iran

Dr. Abol Hassan Danesh

Department of Sociology
Colby College, Waterville, Maine

UNIVERSITY
PRESS OF
AMERICA

Lanham • New York • London

307.2
D179r

British Cataloging in Publication Information Available

Library of Congress Cataloging-in-Publication Data

Danesh, Abol Hassan, 1952-
   Rural cxodus & squatter settlements in
the Third World.

   Bibliography: p.
   1. Rural-urban migration—Iran.   2. Urban—rural
migration—Iran.   3. Urbanization—Iran.   4. Squatter
settlements—Iran.   I. Title.   II. Title: Rural
exodus and squatter settlements in the Third World.
HB2096.4.A3D36   1987   307.2   87-10627
ISBN 0-8191-6443-7 (alk. paper)
ISBN 0-8191-6444-5 (pbk. : alk. paper)

90-7932

To Homeless, to Uprooted Migrants, to True Enemies of Poverty

and Despair, to Revolutionary Hope .... TO LIFE!!

ACKNOWLEDGEMENTS

This book embodies more than 9 years of my intense intellectual life. From its inception to its final completion I have greatly benefitted from so many diverse peoples and their experiences. My former sociology teachers at the University of California, Riverside; my colleagues at Colby College, my friends and co-workers at Plan and Budget Organization of Iran, my concrete learning from and experiences with squatter dwellers and migrants in Iran, and finally the emotional and financial support from my family have played the most vital role in formulation and evolution of this book. I want to deeply thank them all.

This is the best occasion to extent my deep and honest appreciation to one of my dear colleagues, professor Jonas O. Rosenthal, who despite his very difficult life schedule, read the entire manuscript, polished my writing style, and identified the rough spots in the text. Without his assistance, the quality of this book would have been significantly different.

Edna Bonacich, Ralph Cauron, Robert Hanneman, Terry Kandel, Mark Gottdiener, Maurice Jackson, and Jonathan Turner are my former teachers and have been tremendously helpful in all stages of my intellectual growth and development. I am indebted to all of them for life.

I would also like to thank Grace Von Tobel for her careful proofreading of the text and her excellent drawing of the tables and diagrams. Also, at any time I had difficulties with word-processing or typesetting, Raymond B. Phillips was always there and helped me with a big smile. There are also people who have helped me out when I was in deep personal troubles and needed genuine help and care. Their selfless support helped me tremendously to continue my education and, thus, it has indirectly contributed to the completion of this book. In particular, I want to thank these wonderful people for their spectacular spirit of justice and concern for human race: Carol Cutler, Wanda Clark, Joe Csapo, and Congressman George Brown, Jr.

Sholeh Gheidari Danesh, my wife, was always behind me and spend so many hours alone at home when I was working on various drafts of this book. She gave me the necessary emotional and mental stamina so that I could systematically work on a triple-shift project. My indebtedness to her and to my parents is beyond verbal expression.

Abol Hassan Danesh, March 1987

Colby College--Sociology Department

Waterville, Maine USA

TABLE OF CONTENT

INTRODUCTION

The goal of this work is to address the interrelated questions of urbanization, industrialization, rural-urban migration, and squatter settlements in contemporary developing countries. Emphasis is put on the structural causes of irregular rural-urban migration in Iran during 1900-1983, and these causes have been analyzed and examined at the economic, social, and cultural levels. A necessary comparison between contemporary developing countries and today's developed nations has also been formulated to identify the major divergencies of urbanization and migration in the course of industrialization.

This book is composed of eight chapters and a conclusion. In chapter I, the major theories of urbanization and industrialization have been examined; and it has been suggested that the pattern of industrialization and urbanization in 19th century Europe was fundamentally different from the one in today's developing countries. At the end of this chapter a typology of rural-urban migration is suggested.

Chapter 2 examines the pattern of urbanization since 1900 in Iran. It is suggested that the existing conceptualization of urbanization is not adequate and the study of urbanization in Iran requires one to incorporate other elements of urban growth. In addition, the spatial distribution of population and pattern and intensity of rural-urban migration, are presented in a comparative perspective.

Chapters 3 and 4 uncover the basic causes of rural population displacement before and after the implementation of land reform. These two chapters are the backbone of this research and attempt to identify the unique sources of rural crisis and rural exodus in Iran. A particular emphasis is also put on the role of the state and its policy in the rural economy.

Chapter 5 shifts the analytical focus from the rural to urban places and presents discussions and materials that are pertinent to the peculiarity of urban industrialization in Iran. Productivity, employment structure, spatial distribution of industries, elasticity of response to unemployed rural migrants in the secondary sector of economy are discussed before and after the 1979 Iranian revolution.

Chapter 6 primarily deals with the non-economic sources of disruptive rural-urban migration. Issues of spatial distribution of social amenities, cultural distortion of rural communities, the role of ideology in mobilization of human resources, and the impact of demographic variables on the pattern of rural push and urban pull are discussed and analyzed.

Chapters 7 and 8 change the focus of the study from the causes of irregular rural-urban migration to that of its consequences. Problems of the housing shortage and squatter settlements are specifically analyzed as the most important consequences of irregular rural-urban migration for the urban centers. Several critical multidimensional typologies are also presented to capture the dynamism and complexity of squatter settlement formation in the Third World.

The conclusion, chapter 9, sums up the general findings and provides a number of practical policy recommendations to resolve the growing crisis of irregular rural-urban migration and urbanization in the Third World in general and in Iran in particular.

Throughout this research divergent data resources have been utilized to substantiate the theoretical statements and argumentation. The data are primarily extracted from the following sources: historical data, two field projects conducted by the author in 1983 and 1984 in Iran, restructured census materials from before and after the Iranian revolution, Persian publications not available to the non-Persian speaking audience and social scientists, personal observations, and discussions with Iranian and Latin American experts and leaders.

CHAPTER I

IRREGULAR RURAL-URBAN MIGRATION:
A THEORETICAL DISCUSSION

Many developing nations have been experiencing an unprecedented growth of urban population for the past two decades.[1] Since the early 1970s the trend has accelerated and it is expected that the less developed regions of the world will add about 1 billion urban people to its population in the last quarter of this century as opposed to 400 million people in the preceding quarter. An increment of this magnitude cannot be without far-reaching economic, social, and political consequences. While a part of urban growth is due to an increase in the rate of natural population growth of the cities, the growing influx of migrants from the rural areas in most cases has become the main contributory factor.

Traditionally, the process of industrialization and economic development has been associated with considerable migration to the growing urban centers of labor demand. But the extent of rural-urban migration in recent years has greatly exceeded the capacity of modern industrial urban centers to absorb the influx and as a result the majority of strategic urban centers has been encircled by rising urban unemployment, acute shortage of basic urban amenities, sharpening class cleavages and inequality, and growing over-crowded housing and squatter settlements. The growing presence of migrants in urban areas, particularly if they are unemployed and segregated, has a number of socially, economically, and politically disruptive consequences for the areas of origin and destination as well as for the national and international communities.

More specifically, the internal migration within a nation-state *has three disruptive forms and occurs when there is an acute disjunction between rural push and urban pull:* (1) Rural-urban migration has negative and disruptive effects on the socio-economic organization of the place of origin (e.g., brain drain, flight of young and pioneer rural workers, breakdown in traditional economic and cultural systems of production, distribution, and exchange), while it is beneficial to the very

---

[1] Throughout this book the terms "developing countries," "underdeveloped nations," "less developed societies," and "the Third World" have been used interchangeably. Nonetheless, the term "Third World" has been used more frequently than others in order to emphasize the *qualitative differences* between the experience of industrialization/urbanization in Europe and in Asia.

1

development of urban economy (place of destination). This type of irregular migration is usually predominant when the urban economy is rapidly growing and needs cheap and abundant labor-- type one; (2) Rural-urban migration helps the place of origin to get rid of its surplus population whose marginal productivity has approached zero, while it intensifies the general socio-economic problems of urban regions (e.g., housing crisis, unemployment)-- type 2; (3) Rural-urban migration has disruptive effects on the socio-economic structure of both place of origin and destination (e.g., migration of young, innovative, and educated village dwellers to cities that cannot absorb them)-- type 3; and (4) The effect of rural-urban migration is positive on places of origin and destination. A typical example would be the transfer of surplus rural population to the expanding urban manufacturing activities-- type four. Diagram 1 schematically demonstrates various forms of migration based on the consequences of migrations for the place of origin and destination.

As diagram 1 shows, migration does not always contain disruptive forces per se and it may even be beneficial for the places of origin and destination, but as we will see, disruptive migration, as in type 2 and type 3, has become the dominant form of population displacement in Iran and other contemporary developing countries. Thus, the focus of this study is on the causes and the consequences of IRREGULAR RURAL-URBAN MIGRATION as a particular and yet important form of population displacement which is not in harmony with the objectives of well integrated socio-economic development and growth.

Much of accumulated theories and research has primarily been concerned with the causes of migration per se and as a result the study of irregular migration has remained in an infantile stage of theoretical treatment. Although many scholars agree that the volume of rural-urban migration is extraordinarily high in the cities of developing countries, they do not present a systematic analysis of this growing crisis. This needs elaboration.

The existing theories of migration such as Ravenstein's Laws of Migration, Lee's Theory of Migration, Lewis-Fei-Ranis' Model of Development, Sjaastad's Human Investment Theory of Migration, Todaro's Model of Rural-Urban Migration, and Castells' Theory of Social Production of Urban Space, at the risk of some oversimplication, can be classified into two major camps: a. Urban Pull Perspective; b. Rural Push Perspective. Although there are some differences within and overlaps between push and pull perspective, each paradigm views the problem of rural exodus with a particular emphasis.

Diagram 1

Typology of the Consequences of Rural-Urban Migration for the Place of Origin and Destination

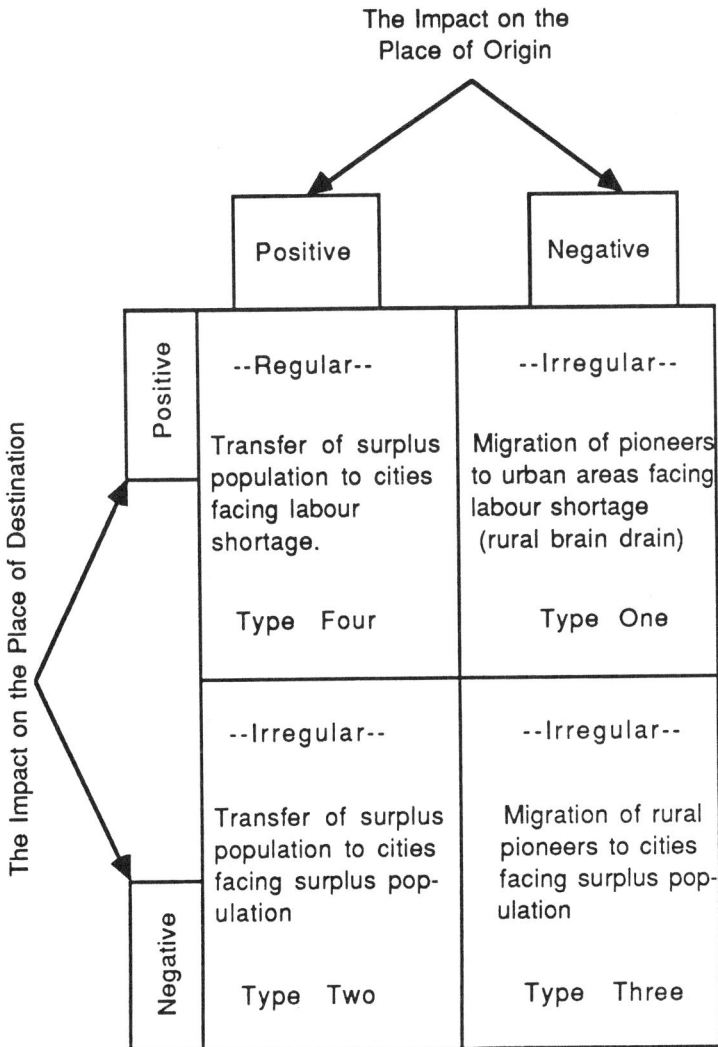

The Impact on the
Place of Origin

	Positive	Negative
Positive	--Regular-- Transfer of surplus population to cities facing labour shortage. Type Four	--Irregular-- Migration of pioneers to urban areas facing labour shortage (rural brain drain) Type One
Negative	--Irregular-- Transfer of surplus population to cities facing surplus population Type Two	--Irregular-- Migration of rural pioneers to cities facing surplus population Type Three

The Impact on the Place of Destination

A number of scholars consider the "urban pull" to be the real cause of migration. They usually argue that possibilities of higher paying jobs, access to a better education as a formal means of social mobility, and absence of rigid social norms and values characterize the urban centers that "pull" rural residents to the cities (N.V. Sovani, 1964:118-119; J. Nelson, 1970:11; W. Mangin, 1967:66). The arguments for the pull factors therefore rest on the increased opportunities for jobs and social services; the new opportunities, in turn, are created by the demand of growing industries for cheap and abundant labor.

On the other hand, some writers put the theoretical emphasis on the changing socio-economic conditions of rural regions and believe that the real causes of migration must be found not in the cities but in the villages that uproot rural dwellers and "push" them towards the cities. The exponents of the "Rural Push" Theory often back up their position by listing and analyzing the high levels of urban unemployment, the excessive growth of the tertiary sector (characterized by low marginal productivity and redundant and odd jobs), and a sharp decline in the standard of living in rural areas (rural poverty). In sum, the Push Perspective stresses the processes of "agricultural decomposition" by looking at how capitalism in general and capitalist agriculture in particular penetrate and decompose rural socio-economic systems and how these changes, in turn, cause displacement of peasants from their subsistence farming. Since the displaced peasants typically cannot find jobs as wage laborers in the countryside, their economic condition is presumed to be the main source of rapid rural-urban migration. Both the Dependency School of A. G. Frank and the World System of M. Wallerstein, which usually emphasize the process of transfer of "surplus value" from non-capitalist sectors to capitalist sectors at the regional, national, and international levels, can be classified as the Push Theory of rural exodus (Castells, 1979:46-48; L. Lomnitz, 1977:41; Morse, 1962; Griffin, 1976).

There are some major conceptual problems with both "urban pull" and "rural push" theories of rural-urban migration as they are applied to the question of irregular rural exodus. First, the push and pull theories of migration are too economistic in their outlook. While this study will dwell extensively on the economic determinants of irregular migration, a conscious effort will be made to understand the social and cultural forces of migration as well. Second, a comprehensive study of irregular rural-urban migration should ideally incorporate into a unitary schema both pull and push forces in the place of origin and destination. Even Lee, who has been cautious to use both forces in a theory, overemphasizes the explanatory power of urban pull in his later writings. Third, both perspectives have failed to identify systematically all the major forces of migration both in the countryside and in the cities. Thus, in the following pages the most critical shortcomings and

4

deficiencies of pull and push theories of irregular migration will be presented and then an attempt will be undertaken to provide a new analysis of migration which is more comprehensive and more practical for cross-cultural research and planning.

Urban Pull Theory of Irregular Rural-Urban Migration: A Critique

Exponents of the "urban pull" thesis explain the phenomenon of rapid rural-urban migration by focusing on the structure of the urban sector and the way in which it has been related to employment opportunities. Factors such as high-paying occupations in cities and the cultural diversity of urban life (e.g., the city lights effects) are seen as the main causes of migration. In pull perspective there is an implicit and unspoken assumption that the migrants are economically rational and make essentially rational choices as they decide to reside in the cities. It follows then that those who can respond positively to economic opportunities are the ones who actually leave the countryside. Thus, the writers often incorporate the factors of "selectivity" into the migration analyses and argue that migrants tend to be more educated, more ambitious, single, and younger than the non-migrants. In other words, the factors of selectivity and the growing urban opportunities are viewed as the fundamental forces of migration that operate somewhat independent of the influences exerted by rural push elements. These two conditions determine who will migrate, and hence, how many. However, with demographic transition and diffusion of mass media and education, increasing numbers fall in the "selected categories" (Sovani, 1964:118-119).

There are a number of serious deficiencies in the urban pull thesis. Fundamentally, the pull thesis is an uncritical borrowing from the European experience of industrialization and urbanization. In contrast to the situation in earlier stages of industrialization and urbanization, the volume of out-migration has become relatively high in the underdeveloped countries while there is no second American continent to be "discovered" which can shelter the surplus. Davis, for example, has pointed out that the growth rates of cities in less developed countries in the 1940s and 1950s were much greater than they had ever been in the history of most industrialized countries. The average annual increase in urban population in those decades was 4.3 percent in twelve countries of Latin America. In contrast, in nine European countries during their period of fastest urban population growth (mostly in the latter half of the 19th century), the average gain per year was only 2.1 percent (Davis, 1965:49).

5

The Iranian case of migration in Asia also shows a similar problem. During 1956-1976, urban regions experienced a 4.6 percent annual increase in population. However, in most recent times, namely after the 1979 Iranian Revolution, the growth rate increased even at a faster speed.

According to the author's calculation, which is based on an urban numeration conducted by the Islamic government in 1983, during 1976-1982, the annual growth rate of cities jumped sharply to a frightening figure of 6 percent. As far as "absolute" figures are concerned, during 1956-1982 the total urban population increased from 9.8 million to 23.2 million people. Both figures of urban growth rate in the Iranian case are way above the rate calculated by Davis for other less developed nations. From these staggering figures one may ask a legitimate question of whether or not these excessive urban growth rates in the underdeveloped countries have anything to do with economic development and urban opportunities, as the urban pull theorists claim.

According to pull theory, one of the primary causes of rural out-migration is the expansion and growth of urban industrial sectors. That is to say, urban growth is dependent upon industrial growth expressed in the relative rise of industrial employment vis-a-vis employment in other sectors of a national economy. A close examination of intersectoral employment in Iran, however, does not validate the theoretical prediction of pull perspective. The available statistics suggest that urbanization in Iran and in other underdeveloped countries is not a replica of the process experienced by today's advanced industrial nations.

The data speak for themselves. In Latin America as a whole, the urban population rose from 29.5 percent in the year 1925 to 40.1 percent in 1969, while the percentage of active population employed in the manufacturing sector remained practically stable from 13.7 percent to 13.4 (Cardoso, 1968). Similarly, in the Iranian case of urbanization/industrialization the share of manufacturing employment did not increase in the face of rapid population growth in the urban centers. In fact contrary to pull thesis the relative share of manufacturing employment remained stable in the nation and actually declined in the urban centers during 1966-1976. It is important to bear in mind that during this period a great volume of petro dollars was injected into the urban economy, a necessary capital formation for economic modernization and growth that many developing nations lack.

Organizing the employment structure of Iran in terms of region (rural, urban, and national) and economic sector (agriculture-mining-extraction, manufacturing, construction, and service), available data reveal that in 1969, the share of manufacturing employment relative to total employment was 18.5 percent. By the year 1976, the share remained quite stagnant, showing only 0.4 percent growth. If one limits the statistics only to the urban centers, the picture of sectoral

6

employment turns into a nightmare. In 1966, the share of manufacturing employment of the total urban employment was 27.7 percent. This figure decreased in the subsequent years so that in the year 1976 the manufacturing employment was 21.5 percent. The existing statistics on the behavior of urban economy, thus, provides a totally different picture from the one presented by the "pull" advocates. Table 1 demonstrates this pattern of urban employment for two periods.

Historically, in most of today's developed countries there has been a close correlation between the process of urbanization and the

Table 1

The Distribution of Employed Population of 10 Years of Age or More in Four Major Sectors of Economy in Iran: 1966, 1976

Region/Sector	Agriculture, Mine & Extraction	Manufacturing	Construction	Service	Total
Year: 1966					
Urban	7.9	27.7	10.2	54.2	100
Rural	70.4	12.8	5.7	11.1	100
Urban & Rural	46.6	18.5	7.4	27.5	100
Year:1976					
Urban	6.9	21.5	13.6	58.0	100
Rural	59.4	16.6	13.2	10.8	100
Urban & Rural	34.9	18.9	13.4	32.8	100

Source: Calculated from Iranian Census Data, 1966, 1976

7

process of industrialization. To express it more concretely, one of the chief characteristics of urbanization has been a rapid growth of employment in the manufacturing sector. Our empirical findings on the relations of manufacturing employment with that of urbanization in the case of selected advanced industrial nations, Latin America, and Iran fit quite consistently with the theoretical statement made earlier here. The developing nations in the 19th century at the time of "industrial take-off", where approximately 50 percent of the labor force was engaged in agricultural activities, had a full grown industrial sector with growing employment in the manufacturing activities. However, in the case of 20th century developing countries, specifically Iran, the same relation has not been reproduced. That is to say, in the latter developing countries the manufacturing sector is weak, due to a number of socio-economic variables which will be identified in chapter 5, and is unable to absorb the structural shocks generated by the rapid changes in the sectoral composition of traditional economy.

Table 2 demonstrates that Austria, France, Italy, USA, and Ireland, as selected examples of developing countries which stood at the threshold of "industrial take-off" in mid 19th century, generated a relatively high level of employment in the manufacturing sector. The shares of employment in this sector from the total employment were 28, 29, 34, 25, and 34 percent in the respective countries. In the cases of Brazil, Mexico, Peru, and Iran, however, the share of manufacturing employment, at the corresponding level of agricultural employment calculated for the advanced industrial nations in mid-19th century, was quite low. It was 13 percent in Brazil in 1960, 17 percent in Mexico in 1960, 15 percent in Peru in 1960, and 13.8 percent in Iran in 1956.

Ironically for the pull advocates, in the subsequent years of urbanization/industrialization in Iran after 1956, the decline in the relative share of employment in agriculture led to the tertiarization of urban economy. Service and construction sectors had the greatest growth amongst all economic sectors and the manufacturing sector which is the heart and wheel of industrialization remained quite stagnant. In order to take a meaningful picture from the behaviour of the industrial sector, it is crucial to separate the secondary sector into two sub-sectors, namely manufacturing and construction. Otherwise, the growth of employment in the construction sector, even when there is a decline in the share of employment in the manufacturing sector, will be interpreted as an indicator of industrialization.

It is now necessary to examine the nature of the the tertiary sector and see how the unique pattern of urbanization and industrialization in Iran conditions its form and its content. The tertiary sector (service) in Iran shows an extraordinary growth and expansion since 1956 and

8

Table 2

Sectoral Composition of Labour Force in the 19th and 20th Century Developing Countries at the Time of Industrial Take-Off (50-54 percent of labour force in agriculture)

Country	Year	Agriculture Sector	Manufacturing Sector
Developing Countries in 19th Century:			
Austria	1880	50	28
France	1886	52	29
Italy	1871	52	34
U.S.A.	1880	50	25
Ireland	1841	51	34
Developing Countries in 20th Century			
Brazil	1960	52	13
Mexico	1960	53	17
Peru	1960	54	15
Iran	1956	54	13.8

Source: 1. Manuel Castells, The Urban Question, p. 41.
2. F. H. Cardoso, Industrialization, Occupational Structure, and Social Stratification in Latin America, p. 33.
3. Census Data, Iran, 1956: Statistical Center of Iran.

the expansion itself is more pronounced in the urban centers. During 1956-1976, the relative share of employment in this sector grew from 23.7 to 32.8 percent. Limiting the data only to the urban regions, it was found that the share was 54.2 percent in 1966 and 58 percent in 1976 (Iranian Census Data, 1966, 1976). As far as the experience of European industrialization is concerned, the excessive growth of the tertiary sector occurs not during the industrial take-off but after its completion.[2] In other words, the tertiarization of the economy has become the dominant feature of developing and developed nations in the mid-20th century, while there is no resemblance between their industrial base. This major discrepancy between the developed and the underdeveloped nations has been expressed in Diagram 2.

It is also important to compare the quality of activities in the tertiary sector of developed and underdeveloped nations for the same period. This comparison allows an examination of the nature of employment in the the service sector in which many rural migrants find employment in urban settings. In the developing countries, the tertiary sector is primarily unorganized and mainly consists of small and petty commerce, hawkers, travelling salesmen, unskilled and temporary workers, public and private servants--a disguised form of unemployment, whereas in advanced countries, the tertiary sector is characterized by efficiency and economy of scale. A cross-national comparison of economic productivity of the tertiary sector in Iran and in a selected sample of advanced nations quite clearly backs up this assertion.

First, the tertiary sector in Iran, as in many developing nations, is less productive than its industrial sector. In fact, in 1972, the average marginal productivity of the tertiary sector was 137,000 rials (one dollar is equal 70 to 90 rials) per person whereas in the secondary sector the marginal productivity was 213,000. likewise, at the international level, the United States' tertiary value added per person was 4 times greater than Iran's tertiary value add in 1972. In the case of West Germany and Italy the ratio was 3 to 1 and 2 to 1 for the corresponding nations in 1972.[3]

---

[2] During 1980-1981, the percentage of the labour force in the tertiary sector of advanced countries has been quite high. The tertiary sector in Norway embraced 62 percent of the total labour force, in Sweden, 64 percent, in England 62 percent, in West Germany, 51 percent, in Italy 53 percent, in the US 66 percent, and in France 60 percent. Source: *ILO (World Labor Report) I,* Employment, Income, Social Protections, New Information Technology, pp. 197-203, 1984.

[3]Source: Plan and Budget Organization, Nakhosteen Santeze Etelaat Moojood: Shenasaeey Manateghe Gerehee "Bohranee ya Mosaed. This volume is among 20 volumes of work which were completed by French social scientists. The emphasis is on long term planning with a heavy bias toward French Structuralism. Overall, It is extremely a useful

Diagram 2

The Pattern of Change in the Main Sectors of Developed and Underdeveloped Nations Over Time

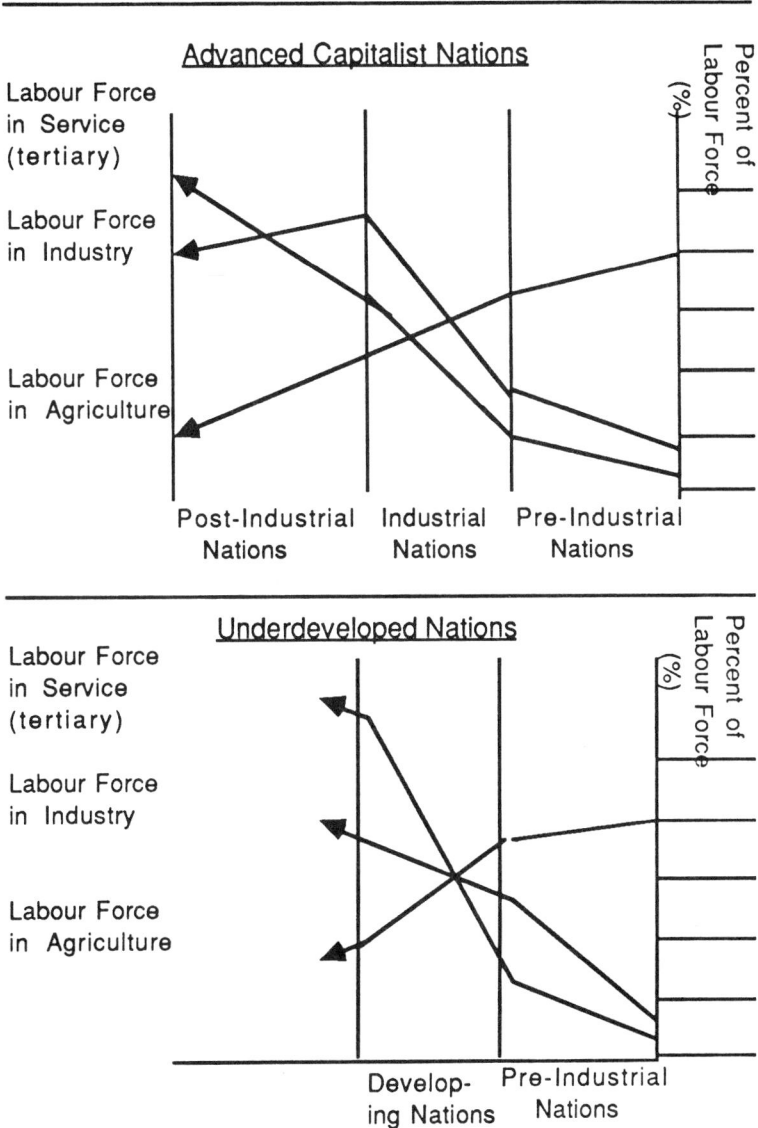

Advanced Capitalist Nations

Labour Force in Service (tertiary)

Labour Force in Industry

Labour Force in Agriculture

Percent of Labour Force (%)

Post-Industrial Nations   Industrial Nations   Pre-Industrial Nations

Underdeveloped Nations

Labour Force in Service (tertiary)

Labour Force in Industry

Labour Force in Agriculture

Percent of Labour Force (%)

Develop-ing Nations   Pre-Industrial Nations

Third, in terms of internal composition of the tertiary sector, the service sector has been developed unevenly. On the one hand, the advanced segment of the service sector, which embraces activities such as banking, commerce, education, police and administration, is not adequate to meet the basic needs of people. The functioning of this subsector is primarily tuned to the needs of an international capitalist system in which the national economy is lodged. On the other hand, the traditional segment of the service sector contains a great number of unskilled laborers with an extraordinarily low productivity. This segment, with little inter-connection with the modern segment of the service sector is made up of a large number of redundant and very small "firms" in which the employees and the employers have very precarious relation with the means of production. This is evidenced by the number of employees in this segment of the service sector. In 1968, the rate for small units was 1.5 persons and for large units 3 persons per firm. In fact, the extraordinary growth of the traditional segment of the service sector has largely been a reaction to the growing rate of urban unemployment generated by the decline in the relative share of employment in the agriculture and manufacturing sectors. For these facts and reasons, thus, it is not justified to call these employment opportunities signs of urban pull in the developing countries. Unfortunately, some advocates of pull theory may like us to see it that way.

In conclusion, the pull theory is not a viable explanation of irregular migration in Iran. After all, the theory predicts that migration is a response to growing opportunities in the urban centers triggered by the expansion of the secondary sector. However, the overall economic structure of Iran for the past 20 years shows that the manufacturing sector has been retarded and the tertiary sector has largely been filled up by illiterate and unskilled rural migrants with low productivity. In many ways, *these jobs are not "there" in the cities to be filled by the migrants but they are in fact "created" by the migrants themselves in a desperate struggle for daily survival.* No wonder we hear and read about frequent and violent clashes between the state's authority and the informal workers in the service sector (certainly, it was the fact of life in the streets of Tehran city). Thus, the waves of rural out-migration are not in correspondence with the needs of cities. After all, the phenomenon of irregular rural-urban migration is an indication of an unhealthy pattern of urbanization. In fact to rely solely on the pull theory as an explanation of the phenomenon of irregular migration begs the very question. This suggests that models based on the European experience of industrialization cannot be applied to the developing nations without more careful consideration.

It is true however that the rural migrants, despite various animosities that they face in the cities, see some improvements in their overall well being. Although the waves of rural-urban migration are disruptive to the general fabric of the cities and usually obstruct a march toward a comprehensive and healthy development and planning at the macro-level, the rural-urban imbalances in terms of the distribution of scarce resources such as shelter, food, and jobs, is so sharp that the act of migration turns into a rational decision at the micro-level for the individual migrant. This means that the differential distribution of opportunity in space (e.g., rural areas versus urban areas, small cities versus large cities) is so unequal that it can compensate even for the loss of expected income incurred during the time of unemployment in the destination. Thus, under constant socio-economic conditions in the place of origin, variations in the value of pull forces in the advanced regions (large cities) explain and predict the rate of rural-urban migration in general and irregular migration in particular.

We will utilize this important insight found in the pull theory in our analysis of regional migration in Iran. That is to say, the notion of urban pull is a relativistic concept in relation to the general socio-economic conditions in the place of origin. Thus, it follows that what is defined as "bad condition" (from the view point of the state's officials, upper class citizens, social engineers and planners) turns into a "good condition" (from the view point of migrants) when it is compared with the "worse condition" (general socio-economic opportunities in the place of origin from the view point of migrants). What is defined as irregular (from the structural point of view) can be redefined as regular (from the standpoint of migrants).

Our next task is to evaluate the competing paradigm, namely rural push theory, and see to what extent it can correct some of the theoretical inconsistencies of the pull legacy.

Rural Push Theory of Irregular Rural-Urban Migration: A Critique

In many ways, the push theory of migration emerged as an alternative explanation of irregular migration. It strived to correct some of the major theoretical and empirical flaws found in pull theory by shifting the conceptual emphasis from the place of destination to the place of origin. In this sense, push theory can be conceived as a rural perspective which tries to comprehend the structural forces which uproot the rural people from their socio-economic niches, and therefore cause some form of "involuntary migrations" towards the cities.

---

research in Iranian studies.

Specifically, in the light of very limited social and economic opportunities in the cities, the push theory attempts to analyze how the intrusion and penetration of modern capitalist social relations into the countryside trigger the waves of rural exodus to the urban centers which themselves have already been suffering from the inadequacy of existing social and economic resources. Manuel Castells, as one of the chief exponents of the contemporary push perspective, summarizes succinctly the causes of migration in a paradoxical form:

> The rush towards the town, in general, regarded much more as the result of a rural "push" than of an urban "pull", that is to say, much more as a decomposition of rural society than as an expression of the dynamism of urban society. The problem is to know why, with the penetration of one social formation by another, a migratory movement is triggered-off, whereas the possibilities of urban employment are well below the dimensions of the migration and the prospects with regard to living standards are very limited (M. Castells, 1979).

Having the aforementioned theoretical thrust, the push theory rather convincingly undermine one of the major assumptions of pull theory, namely the differential income level between the countryside and the city, which presumably "pull" the rural residents to the cities. Todaro in his defense of pull theory claims that despite a high level of unemployment in the cities migrants can afford to remain unemployed for a while in the city because the long run "expected" income in the cities is significantly higher than in the countryside (Todaro, 1969). The push theory would argue against this important assumption of pull theory.

Push theory also considers the existing differential income between the city and the countryside as superficial, fundamentally because the cost of social reproduction of migrants is higher in the city. This differential cost of reproduction therefore cancels out the previous income differential between the countryside and the city. For instance, in rural areas, the place of residence and the place of work are not geographically segregated. The relative spatial proximity between the place of reproduction and the place of production sets free the rural worker from the transportation cost. In the city, in some instances, rural migrants must spend more than 30 percent of their earned income for the cost of transportation, which in turn cancels out the original income differential. Additionally, since the money economy is more pervasive in the cities than in the countryside, cash payment becomes inevitable and necessary for the direct consumption of agricultural and housing commodities in the cities.

Shifting away from economic to cultural determinants of rural-urban migration, the push theory also de-emphasizes the role and significance of cultural pull variables (often cited as the city lights effect), such as diffusion of new urban consumption, attractiveness of western cultural values of individualism and democracy, primarily because these variables cannot be regarded as motive force of the process. The real motive forces of the processes of migration, according to the push perspective, are structural in nature and are not reducible to the psychological make-up of individuals. Furthermore, there has to be a certain level of correspondence between the code of the emitter and the code of the receiver in relation to information message. Thus, as the western cultural system reaches the countryside, it will be transformed, redefined, and "selected" according to the general system of symbols and cultures in the place of origin (rural areas). Specifically, in those cases where they have shown a great level of reception to the western cultural way of living (e.g., mass consumption), it has been found that the traditional cultural system in the rural regions has already been disorganized by the structural basis of the new situation (Barraclough, 1968; M. Castells, 1979).

In sum, neither the differential incomes between the countryside and the city, nor the diffusion of western cultural values can be considered as the main causes of irregular migration. According to push theory, one can conclude that the real causes of rural exodus lie in the very disorganization and breakdown of agrarian society. These fundamental and drastic changes in the socio-economic structure of rural society, according to push advocates, is primarily due to the "contradiction between population growth", a consequence of the recent rise in life expectancy and the maintenance of non-productive "forms of land ownership" (Castells, 1979). Thus, to explain the sources of irregular rural-urban migration, following the push theory, one is encouraged to look at the differential impact of industrialization in rural and urban societies from without, which in turn has produced differential productive capacities in space as the rural economy deteriorates.

To summarize the major theoretical thrust of push theory, one may find the following propositions: (1) The more population growth, the more rural exodus. (2) The more farming land is in the form of non-productive land ownership, the more rural exodus. (3) The more exchange between the countryside and the cities (e.g., new roads, modern means of communications), under the conditions of high population growth and unproductive land tenure, the more rural exodus. (4) The greater the differential productivity in the space (rural vs. urban), the greater the level of migration from the less productive sectors to the more productive sectors.

As these propositions imply, push theory, while correcting some of the major theoretical deficiencies of pull theory, carries its own unique theoretical weaknesses which have been created by an exclusive focus on the rural processes. Confronting the above theoretical propositions of push theory with empirical fact, particularly in the light of new findings in the case of industrialization and migration in Iran, will show the extent to which the push theory can withstand the challenge of theoretical and empirical scrutiny.

First, at the theoretical level, the push theory, to some extent, suffers from the same handicaps that the pull theory does. Both are one sided. Since push theory was formulated as a "reaction" to the deficiencies of pull theory, it remained blind to some of the insightful theoretical discoveries "pulled-out" by the pull advocates. In other words, rural push in and of itself is not a sufficient condition to explain the phenomenon of irregular migration. It does so only in relation to the conditions set by the urban economy and urban social arrangements, namely the factors of selectivity and the changing dynamism of urban labor demand.

Second, at the empirical level, the push advocates have underestimated the capacity of rural settings in absorbing some portions of surplus population. Push theory ascribes much of the rural exodus to the traditional organization of land tenure and its level of productivity (proposition 2). Although this element is one of the major and critical factors of out-migration, the available statistics on the size and growth of rural population in the developing countries in general and in Iran in particular, demonstrate that rural systems in their present forms has a surprising capacity to produce job and to sustain a great number of human lives. Rural sectors in the developing countries do not experience a rapid decline in the absolute size of population. Contrary to common belief and superficial observation, villages in the developing countries are not like what Goldsmith describes in his "The Deserted Village." He says:

> But now the sounds of population fail, No cheerful murmurs fluctuate in the gale, No busy steps the grass-grown footway treated, For all the bloomy flush of life is fled.

The available information on the pattern of population composition and population growth in the rural regions of the developing countries tells us that while rural population is increasing at a slower rate than the urban population, the rural population in this part of the world has experienced a very substantial absolute increase in size, from 1.4 billion in 1950 to an expected 2.8 billion by the turn of the 21st century. According to the available projections, the rural population in the developing countries at the turn of the next century will equal what the total population of developing countries was in 1975.[4]

Specifically, in the case of Iran, rural regions demonstrate a relatively high level of population growth in addition to the high current

---

[4]Source: United Nations, Patterns of Urban and Rural Population Growth, Population Studies, no. 68, New York, United Nations, 1980.

level of rural-urban migration. By the end of the year 2000, the United Nations has estimated that the Iranian rural regions will contain as much as twofold of its rural population in the year 1950. Plan and Budget Organization of Iran also shows that during 1963-1975, in addition to the rural population which left the countryside, more than four million eighty-six thousand individuals were added to the existing 14.57 million rural residents in 1963 (Economic Trends of Iran, 1978). In terms of agricultural employment, which is concentrated in rural areas, the available statistics also show that instead of decline, the absolute size of agricultural employment has been constant during 1957-1977. In 1959, approximately 3.4 million Iranian citizens were engaged in agriculture, the size slightly increased during 1959-1970. In 1970, the total size of farming employment was 3.75 million. After the year 1970, the size of farming employment was reduced and was equal the size of farming employment in 1957. These figures simply tell us that the traditional agrarian economy, in spite of its low productivity and in spite of its economic inefficiencies, has generated a size of employment that is much higher than what push theory advocates have predicted from their theoretical vantage point. In fact, one should expect a greater level of rural push and a higher level of irregular rural-urban migration in the developing countries if a full fledged capitalist agriculture is going to take place. For instance, the United States experienced a high level of capitalist penetration in its countryside. Much work was taken up by the growing high labor-saving technology. The net result was a rapid decline in the absolute size of farm population. The United States contained approximately 44 percent of its entire labor force in farming and related activities in the late 19th century. By the year 1980, the extensive use of modern farm technology reduced the share of farming employment to only 4 percent of the entire labor force.

Third, the rural push does not invariably cause various social groupings to move towards the city. Major findings on the characteristics of migrants in Iran and in other developing countries show that age, marital status, economic status, education, and sex differences generate differential resistance to rural push. In the case of Iran it was found that younger rural residents were more vulnerable to rural push than older ones, perhaps because they cannot acquire land due to inheritance. The most recent census data showed that more than 75 percent of migrants who settled in Tehran city during 1971-1976 were between 15 to 35 years of age. Similarly, single rural residents were less resistant to the worsening rural conditions than the married dwellers, presumably because they had more choices and were equipped better to deal with a new environment in the place of destination. Usually, in hard times, more social and cultural support is given to married people with children than to the single dwellers, and the latter are encouraged by their families and peers to migrate in order to make life easier for the remaining village dwellers who are more vulnerable to economic crises.

17

Thus, it seems to be ironical for push theory to see that those who have the least options and are more vulnerable to socio-economic crisis(the author exclusively means married people with children) are likely to stay in the countryside and to fight back the deteriorating conditions in their villages by capitalizing on the existing cultural support system found in their villages. More elaboration will be made on the cultural aspect of migration in chapter 6.

In terms of rural exodus and sex, the available statistics also showed that men tend to be more prepared for migration than women. Given the extreme dependency of women on their male kin, namely brother, father, uncle, and husband, for economic and social survival in Iranian society, the aforementioned relation should be understood with no difficulty. Interestingly, it was found among migrants to Tehran city that the sex ratio increased as the distance between the place of origin and Tehran city increased. Thus, in order to explain why the rural residents come to the cities where there are no social and economic opportunities, one must break down the question for various socio-economic groupings and then analyze how they differentially respond to rural push as well as urban pull variables.

It is, thus, suggested that the incorporation of selective factors as intervening variables into the theory of rural push will improve its degree of predictability and its ability tell us who will likely leave the countryside as the rural push becomes stronger.

Finally, a high level of rural push in and of itself does not generate irregular migration. It depends on the extent to which urban sectors can respond to the deteriorating conditions in the rural sectors. Thus, under those conditions where the urban economy is doing well and its dynamic sectors produce an adequate number of employment opportunities that fit the general qualifications of rural migrants, a high level of rural-urban migration will not be a disruptive force and it cannot be considered as "irregular migration."

For example, some of today's developed countries experienced a tremendous rural push. However, this condition did not set forth the forces for the release of irregular rural-urban migration. In fact, due to the growing labor intensive factories in urban sectors, many pushed-out migrants were absorbed by the urban economy. The best example is the case of industrialization, migration, and urbanization in Japan. The low level of urban pull "alone" is also not a sufficient condition for the growth of irregular rural-urban migration. The level depends on the general conditions (social, economic, cultural, political) in rural areas. It follows that in those cases of industrialization where the rural push is not very high and contains forces that do not allow for a high level of out-migration, despite the weakness of the urban economy, migration tends to be regular and not disruptive to either rural or urban regions (e.g., industrialization in China, Albania, and Scandinavian countries).

Diagram 3

Typology of Rural-Urban Migration Based on the Volume of Rural Push and Urban Pull

RURAL PUSH

	LOW	HIGH
LOW	Regular Migration (e.g., China)	Irregular Migration (e.g., Iran)
HIGH	Regular Migration (e.g., USA)	Irregular Migration (e.g., Japan)

URBAN PULL

Notation: This typology only shows the general characteristics of migration in various societies. Of course, there are some significant variations within each type. In the case of Iran, for example, in accordance with the long term goals of socio-economic developement, one can empirically demonstrate some significant variations across different regions. In other words, if one changes the unit of analysis from the nation-states to that of local regions within a given national-state, all these four major types of migration, of course with differential frequencies, will be applicable to Iranian society.

Thus the rural-urban migration turns into an irregular migration "only" when there is a *significant and acute discrepancy between the level of rural push and the level of urban pull*. That is to say, when the level of rural push is high but the level of urban pull is low, it is expected that much of the internal migration from rural to urban regions would become irregular. From this theoretical choice it follows that: (1) Rural push and urban pull must simultaneously be taken into consideration in order to explain the conditions under which irregular migration is likely to take place; (2) Neither rural push nor urban pull has absolute meaning. Instead, the meaning and its time-bound significance can be explicated only in relation to the other component of irregular migration. A four-fold typology (Diagram 3) schematically demonstrates the intricate relations of rural push, urban pull, and irregular migration.

At such a level of abstraction and complexity, it is not possible to make general and yet useful statements and therefore we should address ourselves to an analysis of a concrete situation. In the next chapters, the meaning and peculiarities of urbanization in Iran since 1900 will be identified and explained in order to understand why rural-urban migration is irregular, what factors have produced the current situation and what can be done about it.

CHAPTER II

PATTERNS OF URBANIZATION & MIGRATION IN IRAN SINCE 1900

Iranian society, like many late developing countries, has fundamentally been altered by urbanization. In this chapter, the trends and composition of this transformation will be studied. It will be argued that it is not enough to simply compare levels and rates of "urbanization" across LDCs and earlier developing nations. Not only are the volume and the rates quite different, but the composition of urbanization trends in LDCs is quite complex, as it may well have been in non LDCs; phenomena at this second level of the composition of urbanization figures may be very important. Therefore it is necessary to identify and evaluate the components of rapid urbanization by using the Iranian case to illustrate the complexity of urbanization in LDCs. This will demonstrate how patterns of growth, levels of urbanization, and the specific composition of urbanization differ in the Iranian case. To accomplish such a task, we should first address the meaning of the term urbanization.

What Is Urbanization?

A look at the available introductory sociology text books and texts on urbanization shows that there is a jungle of definitions for the term urbanization, but one can extract two fundamentally opposite extremes among them: 1. urbanization as the spatial concentration of human beings beyond a certain level of size and density which has been accompanied by a considerable level of rural-urban migration; 2. urbanization as the spatial concentration of people who share and develop a uniform cultural profile similar to Western way of living (e.g., anonymity, impersonality in social relations, complex division of labor, and prevalence of secular over sacred concerns).

As was explained in the first chapter, the process of urbanization(concentration of population caused by rural-urban migration) need not always be associated with the process of industrialization (rise in manufacturing employment) and Westernization. In fact an

21

absence of a clear association between concentration of population and industrialization characterizes the main cities in the developing countries in general and in Iran in particular.

It was an ethnocentric bias, found in the work of the Chicago School, particularly in Wirth's theory of "Urbanism as a Way of Life," that assumed that size, heterogeneity, and density generate automatically and universally a certain set of behaviors which will be similar to the Western way of living. It was a non-social theory of culture, whereby a particular type of cultural profile is assumed to emerge under the naturalistic conditions of physical size and density of population. The history of urbanization in Iran, at least, shows that the concentration of population with large size and great heterogeneity does not always lead to the emergence of the Western type of attitudes and behaviors known as "urbanism." The very nature of the Iranian Revolution in 1979 is a historically bold document exposing the fictitiousness and spuriousness of the relationship between urbanization, industrialization, and urbanism.

Thus, in the case of Third World countries where concentration of population has not led to the formation of a particular superstructure, *one should limit the definition of urbanization only to the process of concentration of population in space.*

Despite the conceptual clarity of this definition which provides a wider empirical scope condition, there are some ambiguities over the threshold of population size beyond which a region is defined as urban. That is, what size and what level of concentration of population constitute urbanization (e.g., a rural place becomes an urban place)?

Unfortunately, no collective effort has been made to resolve this problem. The United States census (1961) used the threshold of 2500 inhabitants as the criterion of an urban region. In addition, unincorporated places that have population density of 1,000 or more inhabitants per square mile and are located on the fringe of large urban areas were also classified as urban. The Iranian census in contrast defines the urban areas as those places that have 5000 or more population. However, the Iranian census bureau will upgrade the threshold from 5000 to 10,000 inhabitants for the next national enumeration, which will be taken after the year 1986. Similarly, the European Conference of Statistics at Prague takes 10,000 inhabitants as its criterion of urban place.

In other cases, particularly in Northern Europe, the minimum population standards are either way below or way above the ones just mentioned. In Denmark the minimum is 200, whereas in the Netherlands a minimum population of 20,000 is required for a place to be designated as urban. Whether a place has a local government, and whether it is a chief town in a district, are also used as designators of urban status in various national definitions (G. A. Theodorson,

1969:359,452-453).

Obviously, the varying and idiosyncratic use of criteria and designators of "urban" make international comparisons of national census reports of urban and rural population proportions extremely difficult and have in fact rendered the ideological dualism of rural/urban paradoxical, since an empirical human settlement can simultaneously be defined as urban or rural.

To solve this problem at a practical level is the responsibility of the United Nations, because it is the only organization that can make direct recommendations, on various issues including the measure of urban designation, to all members of the international community without arousing national sentiments. The following is what the United Nations has done in its attempt at bringing about order to this prevailing conceptual chaos.

In the United Nations' studies, estimates are presented based on urban areas designated by the country under review, rather than imposing a uniform set of criteria. Partial justification for this practice is that national statistical offices are in the best position to distinguish between urban and rural areas in their own country. For example, an urban designation typically implies a predominance of non-agricultural activities and therefore such a criterion of economic activity may have to be introduced. An additional justification is that the size and nature of administrative units, which would necessarily form the building blocks of redefined urban areas, vary considerably from country to country, so that true comparability could never be achieved.

Despite some merits found in this definition, to some extent, the United Nations' solution is a political solution, based on the principle of national autonomy, rather than an academic one. Similarly, no universal threshold level of non-agricultural activities is mentioned. The term "predominance" is vague for operationalization purpose and it does not tell us exactly at what percentage share of non-agricultural activities a region is defined as urban. Moreover, the mixing of population-size with economic, political, or cultural criteria of modernism and Westernism do not yield a useful indicator of urbanization, since it confuses urbanism with urbanization.

Given the international root of this problem in which every nation uses its own idiosyncratic population level of urban places, and given the political and academic autonomy of each nation-state in the international community, the following recommendations may be of some use in bringing about a more uniform operational definition for the phenomenon of "urbanization" throughout the international community: (1) In addition to urban criteria used for local and national study, national statistical bureau in each country should be encouraged to report the size of its urban population districts based on an urban

23

criterion used by international agencies. (2) This international urban designator can be calculated as follows: a. list all urban thresholds used by all members of the international community; b. calculate the average and standard deviation of the distribution; c. calculate the the upper limit and lower limit of this average with one standard deviation; this calculated "interval" can be used as a range within which a region regardless of its political, economic, and cultural forms and composition will be defined as urban. (3) The use of this interval as a designator of urban regions will bring more homogeneity in the operational definition of urban regions as it eliminates extreme cases (e.g., 20,000 in the case of Netherlands and 200 in the case of Denmark).

Furthermore, if some nation-states are unwilling to identify their urban region based on the criterion just mentioned, the major international agencies, including the United Nations, can do it for them so that meaningful cross-cultural studies and comparisons on urbanization can be conducted.

Obviously, this task cannot be undertaken without identifying each specific component of urban composition for the entire urban population. In what follows it will be shown that beside natural population growth in urban centers and rural urban-migration, there are also other important components to urban population, most of which are not identified by the available literature. These components must be identified so that a true estimation of the size of urban population as well as of rural-urban migration for international studies can be made. Here the study will be limited to the case of Iranian urbanization and the procedures could be used with some modifications for other nations. In this investigation nine major components of urban populations have been identified.

1. Immigration to Urban Centers

The flow of international migration to the main urban centers of Iran is one of the major factors of urban population growth. By 1976, the volume of international migration to the major Iranian urban centers had been quite conspicuous. In Tehran city alone, the contribution of this factor to urban growth has been significantly higher than any of the inter-state migration.

The census shows that those individuals who resided outside the Iranian national boundary prior to 1971 comprised exactly 13.4 percent of all immigrants settled in Tehran city by the year 1976. The state of East Azarbiajan in Iran is a primary source of immigration to Tehran city vis-a-vis other Iranian states. The percentage contribution of this state to Tehran population in 1976 equalled the percentage contribution of international migration to Tehran city and constituted approximately 13.1 percent.

Of course the significance of the contribution of international migration to urban growth after the 1979 Iranian revolution has declined. But it is important to emphasize that during major Western oriented development and industrialization in the developing countries it is expected that this factor is going to be the major contributory factor to urban population growth, especially in the capital cities.

2. Colonization of Villages by the Cities

For the past two decades some cities have experienced a great level of growth and expansion without having rural-urban migration or major urban population growth in the city itself. Why? In a number of Iranian cities, urban population growth is associated with the expansion of official boundaries. The result is that the cities incorporate and colonize the neighboring villages as their own integral components and in doing so the residents of the villages are added to urban population.

In a sense, the residents of these rural areas "emigrate" to the near-by towering cities without ever changing their place of residence. The influence of this factor on urban growth is more pronounced in the larger cities where they continuously annex the surrounding hinterlands. According to the author's calculation, the "immigration" of non-emigrants (due to the physical incorporation of neighboring villages) has contributed more than 5.5 percent to the overall national urban population growth of Iran during 1966-1977.

3. Population Growth in the Large Villages

In another way, people can "move" from rural to urban areas without ever changing their residence. It appears ironic but it occurs when certain villages exceed the village population threshold and they become new born cities. The sources of population growth in these villages are quite complicated but one can point to the permanent immigration of declining villages' residents to other villages or to the natural population growth of the village itself. Using the urban population threshold of 5000 or more, the calculation shows that in 1981 approximately 34 villages with the population of 177,912 inhabitants in Iran were reclassified as urban regions. Village to village migration, although not very common in Iran, may also reproduce the same relation mentioned above.

The impact of rural reclassification is quite critical to the estimation of the rate of urban growth. During 1966-1976, this factor alone contributed between 10-15 percent to urban growth in Iran. It is the author's understanding that the way in which this factor contributes to the rise of urbanization is not well recognized in the literature. As was explained, the population of these reclassified villages did not emigrate to cities but in contrast, they became urban dwellers in their own villages. This implies that a meaningful measurement of urban population growth must take into account the effect of this factor. That is to say, it is necessary to subtract the effect of this factor from the gross increase of urban population so that one can clearly see the real magnitude of actual emigration from the rural to urban regions. Without these necessary adjustments the rate of rural-urban migration will be greater than the real volume of people who actually left the countrysides and joined the city dwellers.

It is important to note here that when the distribution of villages is such that large villages are more frequent than the small villages, the impact of this contributory factor to urban growth becomes crucial. The reason lies in the fact that large villages can become new urban regions with a small magnitude of population absorption.

For example, in a hypothetical case where there are 10,000 villages with no urban center (urban population =0), and if each of these villages has 4999 inhabitants (according to the Iranian definition of urban regions, places of 5000 inhabitants or more are considered urban regions), and if the natural population growth of each of these villages is only one per 4999 in a month, with zero inter-village migration, a 100 percent rural nation will become a 100 percent urban nation in a matter of a month. This rapid super-urban population growth would be very artificial and in fact is a simple function of sheer physical spatial arrangements of population. In other words, various configuration of villages in size have different implications for the rate of population growth in the urban regions.

According to the available statistics in Iran, approximately 14.8 percent of the increase in Iran's urban population has been due to population in new urban centers during 1966-1976. These new urban centers embraced approximately 891,000 inhabitants in the year 1976.

In Iran, however, the distribution of villages in terms of size is skewed toward the small villages and thus the effect of population growth in large rural areas on the rate of urban population growth is not very strong. Throughout the nation, there were 54,581 villages,

65.6 percent of which had less than 50 households. Villages with 201 households or more (large villages which have the potential to be reclassified as new urban centers) represented only 5.5 percent of all Iranian villages in 1976 (Iranian National Census, 1976).

Thus, in opposite cases where the large size villages are the majority, sociologists and demographers should be aware of the average population of villages . In those villages with large population, approaching the thresholds of 5000 inhabitants, minor population growth has the potential of providing misleading or even false pictures of urbanization trends for policy makers and other concerned audiences.

Unfortunately, the literature on urbanization shows little awareness of the implications of village size configuration for urban trends in the developed and developing countries. It is expected that inadequate attention to the interplay of this factor with urban pattern will continue to provide wrong and distorted pictures for those who heavily rely on empirical data for sociological analyses and interpretations of urbanization and industrialization in the contemporary world.

4. Settlement of Floating Population--
Transhumant Pastoralists

Tribal populations which usually form into transhumant pastoralist societies are classified as rural inhabitants by demographers in Iran. Tribal populations are constantly moving across the country as they exhaust resources in their temporary place of residence. The local Iranian name for these moving societies is "Ashayer" or "Koochnesheenun" and they constitute more than half a million people. In winter they move to southern regions where there is plenty of food and grazing land for their animals. Once they exhaust resources and the heat becomes intolerable the Ashayerans make the necessary preparations to settle in the northern part of the country where leaves and weeds are fresh and the temperature is pleasant. This seasonal circulatory migration is quite consistent over time and is the only means by which the survival of Ashayerans is guaranteed. Ashayerans are also known for their bravery and are often been manipulated by the central government for politcal goals and military purposes.

However, for the past two decades, the Ashayerans have been facing numerous problems in meeting their subsistence survival needs. Privatization of land ownership in recent years has threatened the life and economic bases of Iranian Ashayerans across the country and has significantly limited their access to wide and open landscape which they traditionally used seasonally to migrate. Given the growing social and economic problems of Ashayerans, the Iranian government decided to settle the Ashayerans permanently in either new places or existing villages.

The direct consequence of this policy of the permanent settlement of Ashayerans has been on the rate of population growth in urban and rural regions. The settlement of Iranian Ashayerans has either created new urban centers where there were more than 5000 residents or they have transformed the rural settlements to urban regions by increasing their population beyond the urban population threshold.

Thus, it follows from the Iranian case of the permanent settlement of Ashayerans and other similar floating populations that in those countries where there is a relatively large nomad population, policies that are oriented toward their permanent settlement will have a drastic impact on the composition and trend of urbanization and urban growth.

This recent trend in tribal settlement is one of the contributory factors to the rise of urbanization and urban growth in Iran. A sound measurement or estimation of urban population must carefully take into account this important pattern of population settlement. Otherwise, the rate of rural-urban migration will be inflated and will be mistakenly seen as the source of urban growth in the nation. Unfortunately, no systematic data are available on our Iranian case. Assuming that between 1/2 and 1/4 of all Iranian Ashayerans have been permanently settled, it is expected that between 250,000 and 125,000 nomads have been added to the urban population.

5. Reclassification of Rural Areas as New Urban Regions for Political and Administrative Reasons

There are a number of villages that have not yet met the criterion of urban regions, but continue to be considered as urban regions. These villages serve some important political and administrative functions in their areas of influence. The Statistical Center of Iran considers these villages as urban places, even though the number of residing inhabitants does not meet the criterion of urban regions.

In 1966, there were approximately 270 autonomous urban units throughout the country, 21 units of which had population of below 5000 inhabitants. Nonetheless, these centers were defined as urban centers. In 1976, the number of urban places holding a population of less than 5000 inhabitants increased up to 40 units. Thus, with a simple calculation, assuming that on the average each of these villages had population of between 2000 and 3000, it can be shown that these villages added about 80,000 to 120,000 inhabitants.ne 6etween 0.3 to 0.15 percent of all urban population) to the entire urban population in Iran.

6. Administrative Unification of Neighboring Villages

Urban population can also increase not because of the natural population growth of urban centers or rural-urban migration but because of unification of a number of adjunct villages into a larger unit having more than 5000 inhabitants. For either planning purposes or for a more efficient administration, numbers of villages may be bunched together into a new unit usually of an urban character (5000 or more inhabitants). Without any change in the social, economic, or demographic features of these villages, these inhabitants of rural places now are considered urban dwellers, due to new administrative definitions of local boundaries.

Of course this form of urbanization is totally superficial and has nothing to do with either population growth or rural-urban migration as the conventional sources of urban growth. To calculate the size of true rural-urban migration, it is recommended that one should deduct the population of these recently unified villages from the total size of rural-urban migration. Without the adjustment, it is obvious that the residents of these villages will be included as an integral part of rural-urban migration. Unfortunately, no systematic statistics are available on this crucial factor, and therefore the author is in no position to estimate the overall contribution of this factor to the growth of urban population in Iran.

7. Reverse Migration From the Cities to Rural Regions

Although the dominant pattern of migration is from rural to urban regions, in few cases the reverse has been observed also. One of the immediate impacts of the reverse flow of migration is on the size of urban population. However, the effect can either increase or decrease the size of urban population. Transfer of population from urban districts to small size villages would reduce the size of urban population, and transfer of urban population to large size villages can enhance the magnitude of urban population when it causes the host villages to go beyond its rural population threshold.

In the case of Iran, the effect of reverse migration on the composition, size, and volume of urban population has been insignificant

29

since it is a rare demographic phenomenon in Iranian urbanization. However, it remains an important factor of urban trends for those countries that have experienced a great magnitude of reverse migration such as China during the Cultural Revolution. As was indicated earlier, under special circumstances, where the flow of reverse migration is directed towards large size villages, it can ironically increase the volume of urban population.

8. Population Loss and Transformation of Small Cities to Villages

A few small cities can become rural areas as they increasingly lose population to the surrounding areas. This usually happens when cities lose enough population to go below the threshold of urban regions.

This pattern of population displacement is more pronounced in the poverty stricken cities in the southern part of Iran, namely in the state of Sistan-Baluchestan.

The transformation of cities to rural regions has a negative impact on the rate of growth of urbanization. This is a "special" case of reverse migration from urban to rural places in which the migrants never change their place of residence. However, given the dominant pattern of urbanization and urban growth in Iran, such a trend was not dominant and therefore it is not likely to distort the basic trend and composition of urban population in Iran. In other cases, however, the effect might be quite serious and must be taken into consideration.

9. International Migration from the Main Urban Centers

Recently, the international migration from the major cities of developing countries has become a dominant trend. The pattern of migration is usually from the less advanced countries to more advanced nations. This pattern of migration is especially pronounced in those developing countries that have some major economic and/or social crises. After the Islamic revolution in Iran, it has been reported that more than half a million Iranian citizens have immigrated to the United States alone. Studies show that most of the immigrants were residents of large urban centers in Iran and came from a relatively high socio-economic background.

The flow of international migration from the urban centers, thus, has a negative effect on the rate of urbanization in the native country and its effects must be taken into account before one can present numbers on the volume and rate of urban growth in those regions.

In sum, the rate, composition, and trend of urban growth and urbanization do not depend only on rural-urban migration and the natural population growth of urban centers. In fact, the processes are quite complicated and one should pay adequate attention to all the determinants of urban growth and urbanization. A schematic and exhaustive model of urban growth and urbanization demonstrate the positive and negative effects of all identified variables of urbanization to urban growth(see diagram 2.1). After adjusting for these confounding variables, it is now necessary to demonstrate the major trends and characteristics of urban population in Iran and to identify their major discrepancies with the pattern of urbanization in other developed and developing countries.

The General Characteristics of Urbanization in Iran

Rapid urbanization in Iran is a new phenomenon. Prior to World War II, much of the Iranian population was rural and the total population in 1900 was 9.9 million people. From 1900 to 1940, the overall population growth was approximately 4.5 million people. In the year 1900, about 21 percent of the population was in the urban areas and the remaining 79 percent was in rural regions. For forty years, however, the rural-urban composition of population did not change drastically and in 1940, the urabn population comprised about 22 percent of the total population.

After the year 1940, the pattern of urbanization changed rapidly. Suddenly, the balance of population distribution in space shifted toward a greater concentration of population in the urban regions. In 1976, 36 years later, the urban population added up to 46.7 percent of the total Iranian population. During this period, the overall population (rural and urban) reached 33.6 million people, approximately 19 million more than the population in 1940. After the 1979 Islamic revolution, the process of urbanization was enhanced even further. By the year 1982, more than 23 million people lived in the urban centers. That is 7.5 million new urban residents added to the 1976 urban population.

Diagram 2.1

The Determinants of Urban Growth in Iran

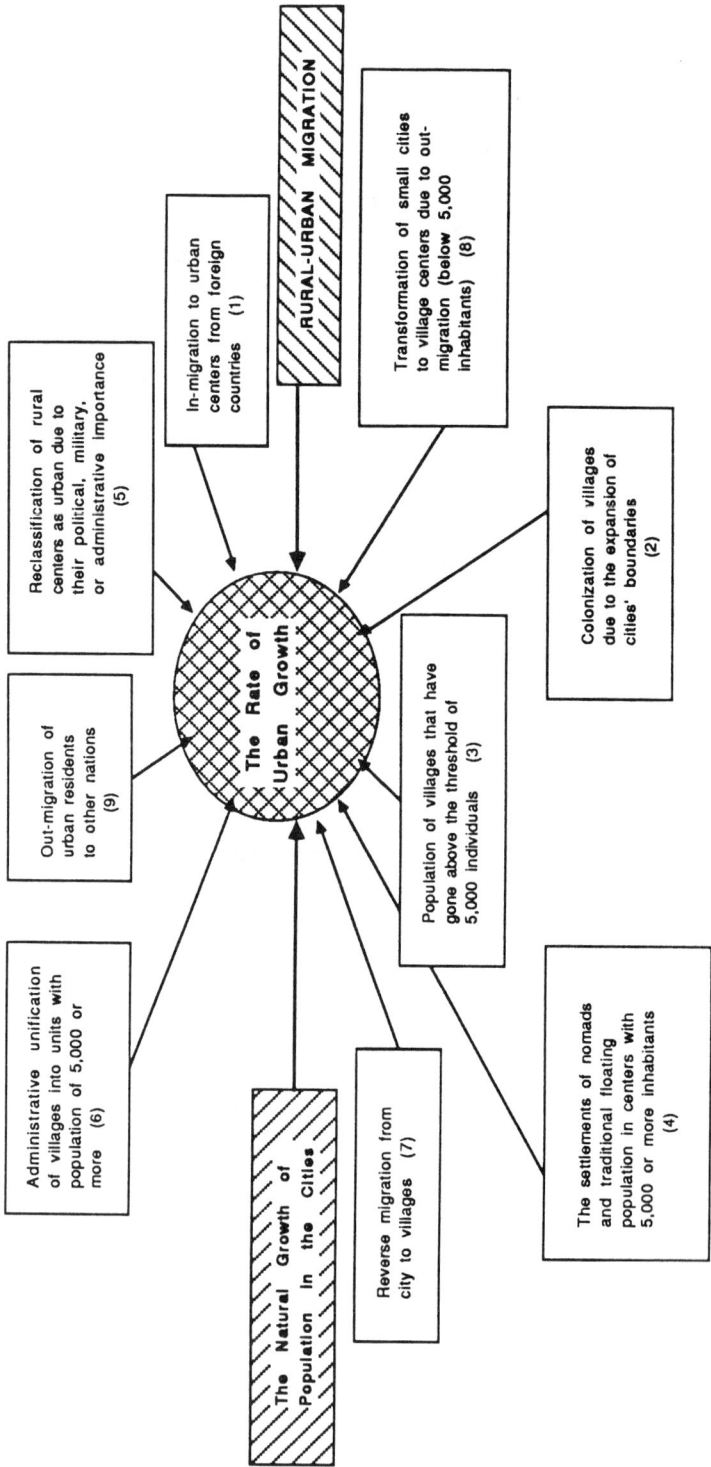

RURAL-URBAN MIGRATION

In-migration to urban centers from foreign countries (1)

Reclassification of rural centers as urban due to their political, military, or administrative importance (5)

Transformation of small cities to village centers due to out-migration (below 5,000 inhabitants) (8)

Colonization of villages due to the expansion of cities' boundaries (2)

Out-migration of urban residents to other nations (9)

The Rate of Urban Growth

Population of villages that have gone above the threshold of 5,000 individuals (3)

Administrative unification of villages into units with population of 5,000 or more (6)

The Natural Growth of Population in the Cities

Reverse migration from city to villages (7)

The settlements of nomads and traditional floating population in centers with 5,000 or more inhabitants (4)

**Urban centers, according to Iranian criterion, have 5,000 or more inhabitants.

Similarly, the rural population grew substantially during 1900-1976. Approximately 10 million people were added to the population of 7 million in 1900. The trend of population growth in rural and urban places both in relative and absolute terms during this period is more vividly expressed in Diagram 2.2.

This diagram makes evident a relatively strong association between process of urbanization and natural population growth. In other words, as the Iranian society approaches the year 2000, a greater percentage of natural population growth will be added to urban centers. A regression equation expresses this finding with greater precision.

Diagram 2.2

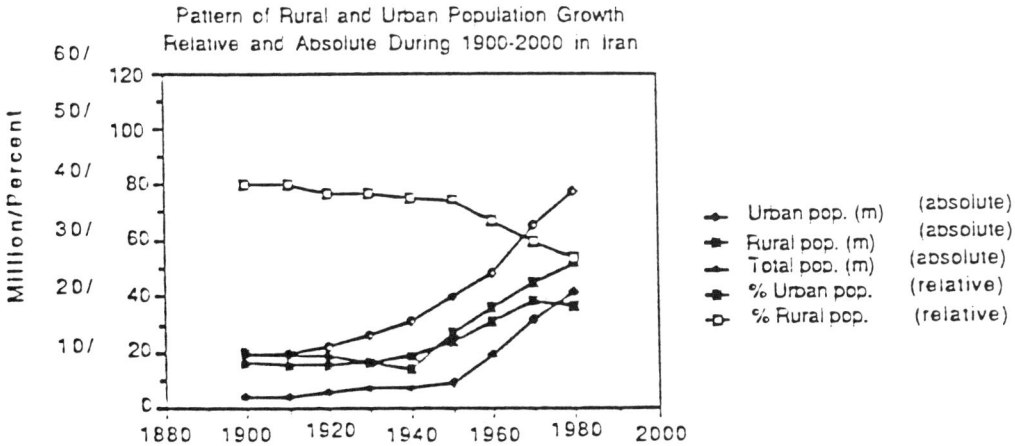

Pattern of Rural and Urban Population Growth
Relative and Absolute During 1900-2000 in Iran

Sources: Adopted from Julian Bharier, _Economic Development in Iran: 1900-1970_ (London: Oxford University Press, 1971); Iran's National Census (1956-66-76); Na-ta-ye-je Tar-ne Ama-re-e: Bar-ra-see-a Masa-ei-e Ko-liee Neey-roy En-sa-nee va Esh-te-ghal Mana-tegh-e Shahree, Ministry of Labour, 1983.

33

If one considers the natural growth of population as the independent variable and the percentage of total population living in the urban centers as the dependent variable, the following regression equation emerges:

(A) $Y = 12.7 + 0.867X$ (during 1900-2000)

The regression equation (A) reveals an interesting relationship. On the average, during 1900-2000, for each unit of increase in the overall population (each unit is equal 1 million), there will be 0.867 unit of increase in the rate of urbanization (percentage of total population living in urban areas). This mathematical relation clearly demonstrates that population growth strongly contributes to the greater level of urbanization. In chapter 6, greater attention will be paid to the role and effect of population growth on irregular migration since population growth goes hand in hand with the rise of urbanization in the developing countries.

To sharpen the interpretive meaning of what was found in regression (A), the regression equation can be specified further for two distinct intervals. The two time intervals are 1900-1940 and 1950-2000. The following regression equations are generated:

(A1) R-square= 0.84, $Y1 = 18.8 + 0.2X1$ (during 1900-1940)

(A2) R-square= 0.95, $Y2 = 10.8 + 0.9X2$ (during 1950-2000)

In the early period of urbanization, as the equation (A1) demonstrates, for each unit of increase in the total population, the rate of urbanization would increase only by 0.2 percent. However, in the later period between 1950-2000, it is expected that for each unit of increase in the total population, the rate of urbanization will increase by 0.9 percent. In a sense, much of the population growth in the rural areas, in the later period, must move toward the urban centers as the rural sectors gradually reach their population saturation level. In other words, the closer we get to the year 2000, the less capable the rural sectors become in terms of absorbing the population growth, and, the greater the level of rural-urban migration. Thus, population growth is one of the major push factors in the villages and its effects for population displacement are greater in the later period of urbanization.

It is also possible to trace the same relationship between population growth and urbanization by comparing the size of urban population over time. In 1900, the size of total urban population was 2.07 million; it rose to 4.88 million in 1950. During 1900-1950, the absolute size of urban population increased by 136 percent. However, the growth rate of the urban population in the years between 1950-2000 period will be further accelerated. By the year 2000, the urban centers are estimated to show 782 percent growth over the population of urban centers in 1950.

Comparing these figures with the trend of population growth and urbanization in other regions of the world, more useful insights can be derived. One of the findings is that the rate of urbanization is closely associated with the pattern of population growth in the rural areas. It has been found that the more developed countries tend to have a low rate of urban growth and a sharp decline in the absolute size of the rural population. In the case of less developed countries the picture is quite different. These nations tend to have a greater rate of urbanization growth and a higher level of growth in the absolute size of rural population.[1]

The United Nations' projection of the world population was used to test the relationship between the pattern of rural and urban population growth for the period of 1950-2000. The data are presented in table 2.1.

Table 2.1 shows that those countries or continents which have scored high on the ranking of the percentage of growth in urban population, tend to score high on the percentage of rural population also. For instance, on the average, all African nations will experience 987 percent growth in the size of their urban population during 1950-2000. This growth of population is the highest growth rate in the world. Africa will experience the greatest rate of growth in the rural population in the world as well during the same time. That is, it is expected that the African nations will experience an average of 150 percent growth in the size of rural population during 1950-2000. This growth rate again is the highest among the selected samples of continents and nations.

In the case of Iran, the rate of urban growth is lower than that of Africa. Thus, it is expected that Iran should score a lower level of growth in the rural sectors as well. The data are quite consistent with this theoretical expectation and show that rural population will grow during 1950-2000 but not as much as Africa's. Similarly, if one ranks the selected samples in terms of rate of rural and urban population growth, it becomes obvious that those cases that were high on the rural

---

[1]However, as the share of urban population to total population increases within each underdeveloped country over time, the percentage growth in the absolute size of rural population will decrease concommitantly. This is probably due to the fact that the more developed countries tend to be more urban and less rural. This relation would imply that the less developed countries will face a greater level of out-migration over time.

Table 2.1

PROJECTION

The Pattern of Population Growth in Rural & Urban Areas in the World During 1950-2000

		Rural 2000-Rural 1950 / Rural 1950	Rank A	Urban 2000-Urban 1950 / Urban 1950	Rank B	A-B
	World	+71%	4	+343%	5	-1
0	More dev. regions	-27%	7	+140%	8	-1
1	Less dev. regions	+100%	2	+669%	3	-1
1	Africa	+150%	1	+987%	1	0
1	Latin Am.	59%	5	+590%	4	1
0	N. Amer.	-5%	6	+120	9	-3
0	Japan	-55%	9	+170%	7	+2
0	USSR	-31%	8	+239%	6	+2
0	Europe	-27%	7	+140%	8	-1
1	Iran	+85%	3	+182%	2	+1

Source: Calculated based on The United Nations' Data, 1980.

Notation: More developed areas and less developed areas are given the value of 0 and 1.

growth were also high on urban growth as well. See table 2.1 again.

To demonstrate the relationship between rural and urban population growth in a more precise and mathematical form, a one way Anova test was carried out for seven cases: Africa, Latin America, Europe, North America, Japan, USSR, and Iran. It has been hypothesized that the more developed nations will score lower on rural and urban population growth than the less developed countries and that the level of development is a powerful predictor of rural and urban population growth level in both developed and developing nations.

The one way Anova test confirmed this hypothesis at the 0.005 level of significance. Data show that the level of development in each region predicts the percentage rate of population growth in rural and urban areas. On the average, less developed countries will experience a 98 percent growth in rural population and a 786.3 percent population growth in the urban areas during 1950-2000. The more developed countries will experience an absolute decline of rural population and a very slow growth in urban population. On the average, the more developed countries will be faced with a 29.5 percent decline in the absolute size of rural population and a 167.2 percent increase in the absolute size of urban population by the year 2000. Table 2.2 summarizes this information.

Thus, from the test of Anova one general conclusion can be made here: the rate of urban growth is predicted to be positively associated with the present rate of "rurality" in today's developing countries.

In the light of this comparative finding which links the level of rurality and development with the growth pattern of urbanization, one must understand the specific expressions of this urban population growth in the developing countries. To pursue this issue, we again need to turn our attention to the peculiarities of urban growth in large cities of Iran in general and in Tehran city in particular.

Tendency Toward a Greater Concentration of Urban Population in Large Cities

The general tendencies of urban population in Iran are characterized by: 1) proliferation of urban centers; and 2) greater level of concentration of urban populations in a few large cities. The number of urban centers in 1956 was 199 units; 10 years later 71 new urban centers had been formed, and by the year 1976 there were 373 urban centers. In other words, in less than 20 years, 274 new urban zones

Table 2.2

One Way ANOVA Test of the Effect of Development on the Percentage Growth of Rural and Urban Population

	Developed A	Less Developed B	One Way ANOVA Test A,B, & F Value	R Square %
Rural	-29.5%	98%	24.65*	83.1
Urban	167.2%	786.3%	37.78*	88.3

*Significant at 0.005 level

Notation: The seven selected cases are mutually exclusive. This choice was made in order to facilitate the use of one way ANOVA test.

emerged, embracing more than 15 million people.

On the average, in 1956, each urban centers represented 30,000 individuals; the figure increased to 36,000 individuals in 1966, and by 1976, each urban center encompassed 42,000 inhabitants. The number of proliferated cities varies inversely with city size. The greater the size of the city the less the proliferation of new and very large urban zones. This pattern is consistent both cross-sectionally and longitudinally. As table 2.3 demonstrates, the number of small cities is larger than the number of large cities in all three periods(1956, 1966, 1976), and the small cities' rate of proliferation is greater than that of the large cities over time. Table 2.3 more clearly demonstrates the pattern of proliferation of cities in various years.

Despite the rapid proliferation of small cities vis-a-vis large cities, larger cities embraced a greater percentage of urban population over time. In 1956, there was only one urban zone with 500,000 or more inhabitants. This urban zone alone represented 25.2 percent of the total urban population. By the year 1966, although no new urban zone with population of a half a million or more emerged, the share increased to 27.2 percent of the total urban population. This trend of regional concentration of urban population was enhanced in the subsequent years as well. In 1976, ten years later, three new urban zones with population of half a million or more were formed and the *four such urban units contained more than 40 percent of the total population.*

The remaining 369 urban zones contained the remaining 60 percent of urban population. Among the four largest cities there has been only one city with a population of one million or more, and this city (Tehran) represented more than 28.5 percent of the total population in 1976.

This general pattern of urban population concentration has been consistent since 1900. That is, each year the share of large cities grows incrementally. It is found that the share of cities with population of over 100,000 has been increased vis-a-vis small cities. In 1900, the total urban population represented 2,070,000 individuals, 24.1 percent of which resided in large cities with population of 100,000 or more. The share of large cities increased to 44.2 percent by the year 1948. The total urban population in the year 1956 numbered approximately 6 million individuals, 52.9 percent of which resided in the large cities of over 100,000 inhabitants. In the subsequent decades, the share of large cities jumped to 57.8 percent and 62.9 percent in 1966 and 1976 respectively.

The pattern of population concentration in relation to city size and time is visually expressed in diagram 2.3. In the next section the nature

Table 2.3
Distribution of Urban Population Based on the Size of Cities in Iran: 1956, 1966, 1976

Pop. Size	No. of Urban Centers 1956	Pop. in Thousands 1956	% Dist. 1956	No. of Urban Centers 1966	Pop. in Thousands 1966	% Dist. 1966	No. of Urban Centers 1976	Pop. in Thousands 1976	% Dist. 1976
10,000	103	671	11.2	139	870	8.9	174	1,180	7.4
10,000 25,000	56	877	14.6	72	1,104	11.3	109	1,649	10.4
25,000 50,000	22	765	13.8	30	1,081	11.2	45	1,540	9.7
50,000 100,000	9	633	10.6	15	1,068	10.9	22	1,532	9.7
100,000 250,000	6	994	16.6	8	1,168	11.9	15	2,153	13.6
250,000 500,000	2	545	9.1	5	1.780	18.2	4	1,345	8.5
500,000	1	1,512	25.2	1	2,720	27.2	4	6,458	40.7
TOTAL	199	5,997	100.0	270	9,790	100.0	373	15,855	100.0

Sources: 1. Iranian National Census, 1956, 1966, 1976; 2. Mohammud Alizadeh and Kazem Kazeroonee, Migration and Urbanization in Iran, B.P.O., 1984, Tehran, Iran (in Persian).

of this urban concentration will be specifically dealt with in the case of Tehran city, and it will be shown that concentration of population in Tehran city deviates from the experiences of developed nations. See Diagram 2.3.

Diagram 2.3

Population Distribution in Cities of 100,000 of More in Iran: 1900-1976

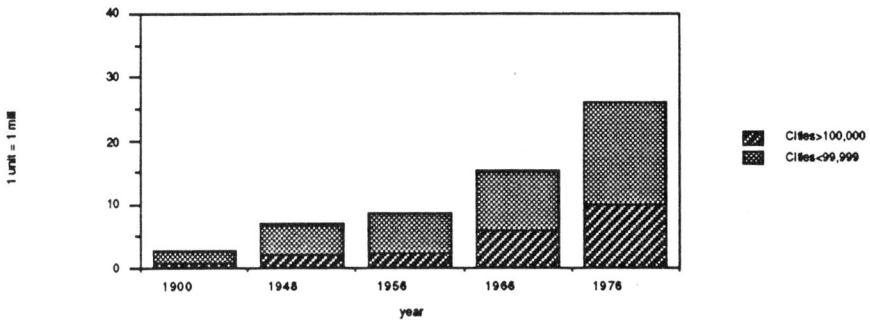

Sources: 1. Iran's National Census, 1956, 1966, 1976.
2. Julian Bharier, "The Growth of Towns and Villages in Iran, 1900-1966," Middle Eastern Studies 8 (January, 1972).
3. Farhad Kazemi, Revolution and Poverty in Iran, (New York: New York University Press, 1980, p. 15.

Tendency Toward the Incremental Concentration
of Urban Population in the Capital City

The process of accelerated urbanization is equivalently associated with the super-growth of population in the primate city. Primate city in the developing countries refers to the largest city in the country, which usually embraces an extraordinary percentage of urban population unknown in the history of urbanization in today's developed nations. It is through the primate city that most of the dependent nations open up relations with the World System's metropolitan nations; also through the primate city, the most remote areas in the hinterland will be indirectly lodged in the wider system of the world economy.

The urban system in the developing countries is characterized by a "macrocephalic" organization whereby the primate city towers and overwhelms the remaining urban districts. In most of the developing countries the primate city is several times larger than the second or the third largest city.

The average rate of primacy can be calculated by dividing the population of the primate city by the population of the second largest city in the country. Brian Berry in his excellent analysis of city-size distributions in 38 countries of the world concludes that the primacy rate tends to correlate positively with the level of political or economic dependency of peripheral nations on the core nations within the world economy (Berry, 1961).

The pattern of population growth in Tehran quite strongly supports Berry's thesis of the primate city. Tehran city was a very small district in 1900. This city represented 9.6 percent of the total urban population. By the year 1944, the share had increased rapidly to 21 percent of total urban population. In the following years, from 1956 through 1979, Iran developed greater relations with the metropolitan nations. During this period the growth of Tehran city was enhanced concommitantly. The total urban population in the year 1956 was four times greater than the overall population in Tehran city. In 1966, the share of Tehran city of the total urban population increased to 27.7 percent. This trend toward the greater concentration of urban population in the primate city increased even further in the subsequent years. In 1976, more than 29 percent of the total urban population was concentrated in Tehran city.

From the year 1956 through the year 1976, the rate of primacy increased quite significantly. Isfahan city is the second largest city in Iran. The population of this city increased rapidly as well, nonetheless it consistently lagged behind the growth of population in Tehran. As a result, the rate of primacy increased over time and the gap between the two cities became wider. This growing gap in both absolute and relative primacy is given visual expression in table 2.4.

Table 2.4 shows that during 1956-1976, the rate of primacy increased from 5.9 to 6.7 units. Likewise, the population gap between the two cities increased in absolute terms. During the same time Tehran city aggravated the population gap between the two cities by more than 2.5 million additional people. While the population of Isfahan tripled during this period, Tehran city increased her population from 1.3 million to that of 3.9 million by the end of 1976.

The United Nations' experts believe that the excessive growth of primate cities in the developing countries has surpassed the limits and it is expected that the rate of primacy would decline in the foreseeable future (UN, 1980). Whether the rate of primacy declines or not, it is a fact that the primate cities in the developing countries have been caught up in a vicious cycle from which, under the present conditions, there is no way out. Although the rate of primacy in Iran is expected to decline to 26 percent by the year 2000, the absolute increase in Tehran population is both inevitable and frightening. According to the UN, it is expected that by the year 2000, 11.3 million residents will breathe from Tehran's oxygen and pollution. In other words, there will be a 916 percent increase in Tehran's population in less than 50 years.[2]

Value of Tehran's primacy will be significantly greater than in most of the developed countries by the year 2000. On the average, the rate of Tehran's primacy will be 2 to 6 times greater than the rate of primacy in such cases as Japan, USA, and USSR by the year 2000. Table 2.5 demonstrates the level of discrepancy among these nations.

We should now look into the pattern of rural-urban migration, since it greatly determines the general pattern of population displacement which is responsible for the organization and reorganization of population in urban areas. The causes of rural-urban migration are diverse, multidimensional, and complex and they will be dealt with in the next chapters. Here the descriptive and quantitative aspects of rural-urban migration are our concern.

---

[2]This figure of urban growth does not seem to be very accurate. During the revolutionary period between 1979-1983, Tehran city has expanded its boundaries to areas designated by the Shah's urban planners not to be filled before the year 2000. Unofficial estimate of Tehran population is about 12 million in 1984.

43

Table 2.4

**Changes in the Rate of Primacy Over Time
During 1956–1976 in Iran**

| Year | Tehran | Isfehan | Rate of Primacy | |
			Absolute (1)–(2)	Relative (1)–(2)
1956	1,512,082	254,708	1,257,374	5.9
1966	2,719,730	424,045	2,295,685	6.4
1976	4,496,159	671,825	3,824,334	6.7

Source: Iranian National Census, 1956, 1966, 1976

Table 2.5

PROJECTION
The Rate of Primacy in Iran and Three
Developed Nations Over Time

Year/Region	1950	1980	2000
Iran Tehran vs. Isfehan	5.6	6.7	6.6
USA N.Y. vs. L.A.	3.0	1.7	1.6
Japan Tokoyo vs. Osaka	1.8	2.1	2.2
USSR Moscow vs. Leningrad	1.9	1.8	1.7

Source: Adopted and Calculated from: United Nations, 1980. Julian Bharier, _Economic Development in Iran: 1900-1970_ (London: Oxford University Press, 1971).

Pattern of Rural-Urban Migration

The rural-urban migration is the first and fundamental force that has shaped the pattern of urbanization in contemporary Iran. Rural migrants do not move evenly into all urban regions and as a result this form of population displacement has been crucial for the growing disparity in the spatial pattern of urban population.

Rural migrants come to the cities either directly or indirectly through a number of moves. The second option is usually open to those migrants who cannot afford to come to large cities at once. Those who are unfamiliar with large cities or do not have relatives and friends to help them at the time of arrival prefer to move to familiar and neighboring small cities. This pattern of migration, known as step migration, is quite common in Iran as it has been in the U.S. among rural southern blacks.

The rural migrants are also a potential force in enhancing the internal migration as a whole in a nation. It has been observed that dwellers in many small and medium size cities move to the larger cities due to the increasing presence of rural migrants in their districts. As the term "step-migration" implies, the rural migrants join the crowds who are in the large cities "step-by-step."

Unfortunately, despite the great importance of rural-urban migration, the Iranian census is not well designed to provide the necessary information on the nature and characteristics of rural-urban migration. Much of our knowledge regarding migration is based on some scattered case studies conducted by Iranian anthropologists. However, the census is quite informative in identifying the regional pattern of "internal migration" within the country and from there some conclusions can be deduced for the pattern of rural migration.

It has been estimated that in the recent years, approximately 50 percent of internal migration is the share of rural-urban migration. Prior to the year 1930, the problem of rural-urban migration was not of a significant importance. Although no direct data are available on this matter, one can interpret and deduce the actual size of rural-urban migration by looking at the annual growth rate of urban sectors. After all, one of the major causes of urban growth is the factor of rural exodus. During the period of 1900-1926, the annual rate of population growth in urban centers was very negligible. It amounted only to 0.08 percent. The rate increased slightly for the period of 1927-1934. According to Julian Bharier, the annual growth rate was 1.5 percent. After the year 1934, one can clearly see a rapid increase in the volume of population growth in the urban centers.

In the subsequent years of 1935-1940, the rate of urban growth jumped to 2.30 percent. The same author has estimated that the rate of annual growth of urban population for the period between 1956-1970 had been quite high, equalling 5.30 percent. On the basis of these data it might be safe to say that the share of rural-urban migration from the overall volume of internal migration increased over time. Julian Bharier believes that in the latter periods (1956-1966), rural-urban migration comprised 90 percent of all total internal migration.[3]

The most direct and accurate data on the volume of rural urban migration can be derived from a nation-wide research conducted by the National Statistical Center of Iran in 1972 (it is not a census). In

---

[3]Probably, Julian Bharier has included the effect of rural reclassification as rural-urban migration; a mistake that occurs very often. In the beginning of this chapter nine variables of urban growth were identified which had nothing to do with rural-urban migration. Thus, if one takes out the effect of rural reclassification, the share of rural-urban migration from the volume of internal migration would be much lower than Bharier's esitmation.

this study it was found that 53.5 percent all internal migration had been the share of rural-urban migration, much smaller than Bharier's estimation. The total volume of internal migration in this period amounted to 3,974,000 people.[4]

The ratio of rural-urban migration to the total internal migration varies significantly for each province. The highest ratio was in the province of West Azarbiajan. For every one hundred migrants in this province there were approximately 71.3 individuals from the rural areas. In contrast, the province of Simnan scored the lowest; 3.3 rural migrants for every 100 internal migrants. The overall volume of internal migration is presented in table 2.6 for three census periods, and shows that the overall dynamism of internal migration has been accelerated.

Table 2.6 demonstrates that there is a positive association between population growth and intensification of internal migration. In 1956, the total population reached 18.95 million people, 11 percent of which were classified as migrants. However, for the next decade, a greater percentage of population was displaced. Out of every one hundred Iranian citizens, 12.85 "people" were considered as migrants. By the year 1976,

Table 2.6

The Pattern of Internal Migration in Iran
(1956, 1966, 1976--in Thousands)

Year	Total Pop.	No. born same place	No. born dif. place-- but same prov.	No. born dif. place & prov.	Total No. Migrants (3)+(4)	% of Migrants (5)/(1)
1956	18,955	16,815	741	1,340	2,081	10.98%
1966	25,079	21,798	1,232	1,991	3,223	12.85%
1976	33,709	25,893	4,392	3,345	7,737	22.95%

Source: Adopted from National Census, Iran, 1956, 1966, 1976

---

[4]In a pilot study conducted by the Statistical Center of Iran in 1974, it was found among 3,341 sample migrants that 66% of all migrants to urban centers had rural origin.

the rate of internal migration reached its peak, growing to 22.95 percent.

Based on the author's calculation, which is adjusted for the contaminating effects of those 9 variables mentioned earlier, about 6,214,000 rural residents join the urban population during 1966-1982. The procedures are as follows:

If:
   p1 = urban population in 1966 (census data)
   p2 = urban population in 1982 (census data)
   r = rate of natural population growth in urban centers
   M = volume of rural out-migration during t1 and t2
   t1 = year 1966
   t2 = year 1982
   N = number of years between t1 and t2

Then:

$$M(t1,t2)= [p2-p1*(1+r)**N]*0.80$$

However: the following data can be extracted from the census:

p2 = 23,236,659; p1 = 9,795,000; r = 0.029; N = 16

Plugging the data into migration formula, M(t1,t2), which is the total volume of rural-urban migration, will be equal 6,214,000 individuals.

In conclusion, the general pattern of urbanization and migration in Iran during 1900-1982 can be characterized as follows: (1) Rapid processes of urbanization unprecedented in the history of urbanization in today's developed nations; (2) A greater degree of concentration of population in the urban regions after the year 1940; (3) Decline in the relative share of rural population vis-a-vis urban population since 1940; (4) Some substantial growth in the absolute size of rural population which have been again unprecedented in the history of urbanization/industrialization in today's developed nations; (5) Uneven distribution of the rapidly urbanized population in the space which accompanied the rapid proliferation of new urban zones; (6) A greater concentration of urban population in the primate city; (7) An excessive natural population growth throughout the nation; (8) And, finally and most importantly, a growing influx of rural migrants to the cities.

In the next two chapters the socio-economic roots of rural-urban migration in rural centers will be identified. It will be shown that much of the rural-urban migration, as the major contributory factor to urban growth in its uneven spatial forms has not been determined by the growing urban economy but has been a reaction to the growing crisis in the socio-economic structure of rural sectors. We must strive, therefore, to understand in great detail the causes and consequences of this component.

CHAPTER III

CLASS AND LAND RELATIONS IN RURAL SOCIETY BEFORE LAND REFORM: RURAL PUSH AND MIGRATION

In conjunction with social and cultural factors, declining rural employment and increasing income inequality are the major economic factors that uproot the rural dweller and trigger migratory movement to the cities. Given that the distribution, ownership, and use of land are essentially interconnected with rural employment patterns and income distribution, a careful study of rural-urban migration in the developing countries should pay attention to changes and continuities in rural-land relations. In many ways, the relation of land to the rural economy is analogous to that of factories to the urban industrial economy. Analytically speaking, the study of land relations in a predominantly agricultural society is like looking at society from a window that highlights the critical components of rural exodus and provides a conceptual edge by which the observer can maintain a sense of direction as one walks into a labrynith of knowledge and empirical investigation.

The land relations in Iran have been subject to great changes for the past three decades, predominantly by the the state's intervention and land reform. Policies which are pursued by the state regarding land reform and land distribution determine the direction of pull and push forces in the countryside. In many instances of "successful land reform," the pattern of irregular migration has been transformed into a more constructive and positive force for national socio-economic development. Thus, the role of state policy regarding land relations can be viewed either as facilitator or resistor to the push factors.

In order to evaluate the impact of land relations on migration, it is necessary to study the relationships among various rural classes be fore and after the land reform in Iran. Such an examination allows one to understand why different rural classes responded differently to rural push and, more specifically, why, how, and under what conditions the privileged classes were able to enhance and solidify their economic interests at the expense of poor peasants.

The Agrarian Class Relations Before the Land Reform

The study of land relations vis-a-vis social classes in rural society is crucial in understanding social change and migration in Iran. First, it specifies the conditions of attachment of the general rural population to the village social milieu, and second it illuminates the differential responses of various rural classes to rural crisis and economic disintegration. The way in which the upper and lower rural classes are attached to the land has a great influence on the organization of production, the nature of class relations, and the flow and circulation of surplus amongst social positions in the rural society of Iran. Generally, in Iran, poor peasants constitute the majority of rural residents, most of whom are completely dispossessed from land ownership. In traditional rural society, the survival of landless peasants was totally dependent upon the decisions of absentee landlords.

The poor peasants can be divided into two major groups: 1) sharecroppers (Nasakhdar), and 2) landless wage laborer (Khushnesheen). The first group has no land of its own but is given the right of cultivation on a relatively permanent basis. The members of this group "enjoy" permanent residency as they are literally attached to the land of absentee landlords. However, their holdings in most villages are subject to periodic redistribution, sometimes by lottery. The main reason behind the periodic redistribution of land is that "the landlord has a vested interest in keeping the allotment of dues proportionate to shares and holdings, and his wish to prevent the sharecroppers from gaining vested interest in his holdings" (Lambton, 1969:26). In a traditional rural economy, the elements and means of production are simple and some sharecroppers may actually own such "items" as seeds, axes, sickles, ploughing cows, and even water. It is obvious that the sharecropper can increase his income whenever he can bring one or more of these items to the land. However, he is still a laborer and must work and sweat on the land.

The second group, khushnesheen, are located at the bottom of the socio-economic hierarchy and in many ways are socially and economically more deprived than the sharecroppers. They are more transient and less attached to the land. The term "khushnesheen" in the Persian language means "no stable residency"; they settle temporarily in places where they feel "comfortable" or where they do not "mind" working. They are a rural proletariat and comprise a great percentage of the rural population. In the early 1960's this group represented more than 33 percent of Iran's total population (Farhad Kazemi, 1980:33). In general, any village dweller who is neither a land-owner nor a sharecropper but engaged in farming and land cultivation is part of the khushnesheen category.

Given the relative detachment of khushnesheen from the land, this group forms the most dynamic population in the countryside. Khushnesheen have been a potential labor force in the past could be readily called upon at the peak of economic activities. Although the khushnesheen had *some secure niches through his landlord's paternalistic networks of loyalty and obligation,* he remained the most vulnerable group in the rural society. Crises in the rural economy first hit the khushnesheen.

Before the 1950's there was not a very significant income differential between the two groups. The main distinguishing factor was one of security. However, the income gap between the sharecroppers and khushnesheen has increased in recent years. During the 1950's the gap between landlords and the lower classes (nasakhdar and khushnesheen) began to widen. Among the lower agrarian classes, a 1954 survey found appalling conditions; locust and clover were the main food supply in a few areas, and the majority of people were seriously diseased. In a later and more comprehensive survey, according to Keddie, it was found that apart from landlord advances, the annual rural interest rate rarely fell below 50 percent. In addition, it was common for a peasant to mortgage his future crop in advance for half the amount he would pay to buy the same amount of grain.

Besides the major rural cultivators and absentee landlord, there were other strata in the villages as well. The main function of these groups was administrative in that they were responsible for control, circulation, and the supervision of rural workers. The bailiffs (mobasher), village headman (kadkhoda), money lenders, and the "Gavaband" were the major components of this intermediary strata between the landlords and the cultivators. Gavabands were distinct from other rural strata in that they usually owned the means of production and some small parcels of land. If the landless peasant or the sharecropper needed tools, ploughs, and seeds they went to the Gavaband. However, since these tools of production were not as important as the land, ownership of them did not give power and authority to the Gavaband. Usually, these intermediary groups owned some land. Although, the small size of their plots was not fundamental to their position in the rural social hierarchy. However, in those instances that they managed to expand their land size, they in fact changed their class position and became members of the small land holder class (malekkiat-e-dehghany or khordeh maliki). There were also artisans, irrigation workers, and local renters whose relations to the organization of production and circulation were not very crucial. By and large, most of these rural groupings had small parcels of land or "nasakh" on which they worked in active agricultural seasons.

The large land holders lived in town and were absentee landlords. Since they were not residing in the villages, they managed their estates through their hired overseers, the bailiffs or "mobasher". Whether the large landlord was a high status military man, an important religious figure, a king or his relatives, government official, or private owner, one fact remains the same--the size of his land was proportionate to the size of his absolute power over the tillers.

Thus the major classes and strata can be defined in relation to the means of production and authority. It is safe to say that the land was the single factor that most differentiated various classes and strata in the rural society. Table 3.1 schematically demonstrates the position and location of various classes and major intermediary strata before the implementation of land reform. These social groups are described in relation to size, economic function, ownership status, place of residency, and political power.

Two years before the implementation of land reform a very comprehensive national survey was carried out to determine and describe the general structure of land distribution among the various rural classes. However, data concerning the relationship between land distribution and the rural classes prior to land reform are more or less unsystematic, subjective, and sometimes speculative, and one should use them carefully.

My analysis of this survey showed that, in 1960 land ownership was highly concentrated in a few hands. There were 1,934,916 rural households. Those households who had access to 5 hectares of land or less comprised more than 63 percent of all the rural population.[1] In other words, these poor rural households together had access only to 19 percent of the total arable land in the country. In contrast, those who had 50 hectares of land or more comprised only 1.15 percent of the total rural households in the nation and allocated more than 13 percent of all arable land to themselves. The landless peasants were in the worst condition. Those who had less than two hectares of land or no land at all comprised 38.1 percent of all rural households in 1960. Altogether, this large and impoverished rural category had access to only 5 percent of 11,356,254 hectares of arable land in 1960. On the average, the share for each household in the group was about 0.76 hectares per household.

These statistics suggest that the land was badly distributed to the extent that a large portion of rural society was landless and at the mercy of landlords. In table 3.2, the distribution of arable land is presented based on the number of households, percentage of households, and size and percentage of land for 5 major categories of land holders: 1) less

---

[1] One hectare = 2.47 American acres.

Table 3.1

Classes and Class Relations in Agrarian Iran Before
the Land Reform Based on Size, Economic Functions
Ownership Status, Residency, and Political Power

Social Grouping	Size	Economic Function	Ownership Status	Place of Residency	Political Power
1. Large Landowners a. Crown b. The Estate (khali'sh) c. Religious Estate (Vaqf)	Very small 1%	Non-Cultivators	Very large land	The City	Very Strong
2. Small Land Holders	Small 5-10%	Non-Cultivators	Moderate scale of landholding	The city and village	Moderate
3. Intermediary Strata a. Bailiffs (Mobasher) b. Village Headman (Kadkhoda) c. Gavaband	10-15% Small-Medium 10-15%	Mostly Non-Cultivators	Occasionally owned a parcel of land or possessed other means of cultivation such as seeds, ox, cows, plough	Village	Weak
4. Rich Peasant	Medium: 15-20%	Cultivators	Owned small pieces of land and use the labour of poor peasants	Village	Very weak
5. Poor Peasant a. Sharecropper	40-60% Very Large	Cultivators	No land but have the right to cultivate	Village	None
b. Khushnesheen	Very Large		No land and no right to cultivate	Village	None

than 2 hectares ; 2) between 2 and 5 hectares; 3) between 5 and 10 hectares; 4) between 10 and 50 hectares; and 5) more than 50 hectares.

To understand more thoroughly the major characteristics of Iranian rural socio-economic structure and their relationship to the land reform and the subsequent migratory flow to the cities, it is necessary to link the pattern of skewed land distribution prior to the land reform with the historical and cultural peculiarities and specifities of rural life. An examination of this link will tell us why land reform was initiated in the first place and in what ways the traditional rural society was transformed.

Characteristics of Villages Prior to Land Reform

In Iranian villages the juridical ownership of land was mainly large in scale, although production actually took place in small units. Whether the land was owned by religious institutions, the royal family, the rich peasants, or traditional landlords, the majority of agricultural production units were small, less than 10 hectares, and the larger units comprised only 17 percent of the available land.

More than 70 percent of arable land was owned and controlled by the absentee landlord who, unlike European aristocrats, resided in the towns.[2]

The predominant trend was that cultivation of land was primarily carried out by the sharecroppers and khushnesheen; owner-cultivators and rural capitalist enterprises were almost non-existent. The predominance of sharecropping over other forms of agricultural production, particularly owner cultivators, significantly inhibited the growth and efficiency of agricultural production. Lack of material incentive for productivity and absence of entrepreneurship and creativity were specifically responsible for the static nature of rural economy prior to land reform.

During this period, most of the Iranian villages were nearly self sufficient and in many instances the utilization of modern technology in

---

[2]It has been argued by many prominent social thinkers that the existence of city feudalism in the Middle East and China was one of the major causes that contributed to the overall stagnation of the rural economy, due to the consumption of rural surplus in the cities. It has also been argued that the presence of landlords in the cities mitigated the independent development of artisans and the urban economy, which led to the overthrow of the feudal system and the establishment of the modern capitalism in Europe (E. Hooglund, 1981:15; N. Keddie, 1968:69).

Table 3.2

The Structure of Land Distribution Based on Households and the Size of Land in Iran: 1960

Rural Classes Based on Land Size	Rural Households Number	Land Distribution Percent	Ave. Hectares	%	Hectares/ Family
Less than 2 hectares	737,099	38.1	570,785	5	0.76
>2–<5 hectares	484,081	25.0	1,553,906	14	3.27
>5–<10 hectares	352,635	18.25	2,413,042	21	10.05
>10–<50 hectares	338,462	17.5	5,263,713	46.5	17.46
More than 50 hectares	21,886	1.15	1,554,808	13.5	124.13
TOTAL	1,934,916	100.00	11,356,254	100.00	6.39

Source: Sar-shoma-ree'e kesha-var-see'e sa-l-e 1339, entesh-a-rat'e ve-za-ra-te kesha-var-se'e. Iran, Tehran.

agriculture was insignificant. It has been estimated that only 4 percent of the land holdings were fully mechanized in 1950's(Bharier, 1971:141). In these villages a money economy was not dominant and the large landholders were solely in charge of the distribution of surplus products throughout the country.

Despite its relatively low level of productivity, the agricultural sector contributed to a great extent to the Gross National Product. Prior to land reform, the primary sector generated more than 33 percent of the GNP (A. Ashraf, 1977:55-58). Additionally, it embraced more than 75 percent of the total economically active population in 1945. The figure is quite impressive by itself, let alone if one compares it with post-land reform in 1967, when only 50 percent of the labor force was in the agriculture sector (Fred Holiday, 1979:173).

One of the reasons that the rural economy could absorb such a great chunk of the labor force was the very nature of villages in Iran. That is, villages tended to proliferate quite systematically in reaction to population pressure caused by a relatively fast rising natural population growth throughout the country. The massive irrigation system, which was unique to Asian agriculture, may be cited as the most critical variable which allowed for village proliferation in Iran. This large scale irrigation system, in the Persian language, is known as Qanat. Qanats are constructed in such a way that they can bring water from a very long distance to remote areas that suffer from land aridity. These water canals are between 5 to 30 miles long.

The available data quite convincingly show a close correlation between the proliferation of villages and population growth and the use of Qanats. In 1900, there were only 3,178 villages throughout Iran. The numbers of villages subsequently increased considerably, and by the year 1956 there were 39,099 autonomous villages. This trend continued and by the year 1966, about 6,034 new villages had sprung up in the dry land of Iran. Most of the villages were relatively small in size and the survival of their residents depended upon the flow of water from the canals. Additionally, given the massive nature of the canals, any time a new canal was constructed, employment opportunities were correspondingly created. Another advantage of Qanats are their function as "fountains of the dry desert." Between the "mother well" which is dug near the mountain water reservoir and the surfacing of water near the village, sometimes more than 200 intermediary wells are dug in order to construct the lengthy underground tunnel through which the stream of water flows. Often, these intermediary wells are used as a ready source of water for desert passengers and their animals who cannot find one drop of water on the hot surface of land in summer. Furthermore, the canals needed repair and cleaning on a relatively permanent basis, which in turn enhanced the pull of the rural society. It is now a bit clearer as to why, despite population growth, rural-urban migration was negligible. In table 3.3 , the phenomenon of village proliferation during 1900-1966 is expressed in terms of absolute and relative rate of reproducibility for five groups of villages (small to large size villages). As the data show, the use of Qanats created differential rates of village reproduction. The rate of reproducibility (proliferation) is higher among the small size villages than the large ones.

Despite the functions that Qanats had for Iranian rural society, it backfired at the political level. In addition to its costly nature, which has been recognized by many prominent scholars (E. Hooglund, 1982:7), many historians and classical social scientists, including Hegel, Marx, and Witfuggel, have strongly argued that the massive irrigation

Table 3.3

The Pattern of Proliferation of Villages in Iran Based on Size and Percentage Distribution Over Time

Year	Village Size	Number of Villages	Percent
1900	2,500–4,999	87	3
	1,000–2,499	307	10
	500–999	398	12
	250–499	634	20
	50–249	1,752	55
TOTAL		3,178	100
1956	2,500–4,999	256	1
	1,000–2,499	1,682	4
	500–999	4,314	11
	250–499	8,931	23
	50–249	2,321	61
TOTAL		39,099	100
1966	2,500–4,999	598	1
	1,000–2,499	1,863	4
	500–999	5,170	11
	250–499	10,140	23
	50–249	27,876	61
TOTAL		45,133	100

Source: Calculated and adapted from:

1. Iranian National Census, 1956, 1966.
2. Julian Bharier, Economic Development in Iran: 1900-1970 (London: Oxford University Press, 1971).

system, which was constructed only with the financial support (and therefore political intervention of the state), caused the formation of a rigid and change-resistant socio-political system known as "Asiatic Despotism."[3]

The Iranian situation more or less fits the description of Asiatic Despotism.[4]

The existence of a powerful functional bureaucracy and a central army in the old Persian empire, which began some 3000 years ago, is a historical fact. Also, the arbitrary use of power by the king is well documented in the history of major dynasties. Iranian history is filled with cruelty and despotic control. A glance at the deeds of famous Persian kings such as Nader Shah, Shah Abbas, and Agha Mohammad Khan Ghajar proves the point.

Agha Mohammad Khan Ghajar, the founder of the Ghajar dynasty, pulled out 50,000 pairs of eyes and he blinded nearly all the residents of Kerman city for their resistance to his rule. In Persian poetry, the city of Kerman and the city of the blind have in fact been used interchangeably. Similarly, Shah Abbas was exceptionally brutal to his political opponents. He would bring his enemies "to their knees" by forcing them to "drink" melted lead from a funnel. One could go on to list 1000 more similar cases to show the centrality, abuse, and arbitrary nature of political power in Iranian society.[5]

---

[3]The Asian villages, because of their excessive reliance on heavy irrigation, were different from their European counterparts in terms of their basic socio-cultural characteristics. Some of these characteristics are summarized as follows: 1. absence of private property; 2. retention by the village community of as essential cohesive force which withstood the bloodiest of conquests through centuries; 3. close union of agriculture and craft industries reenforced by 1 and 2; 4. a more collective form of farming was encouraged; and finally 5. state concentration of the greater portion of surplus for its own use, which caused in turn the hypertrophied and despotic character of the state.

[4]Henri Goblot argues that the Iranian rural society cannot be considered as a despotic society because most of the irrigation projects were small scale and thus completed by the local residents independent from the state's resources. In addition, an irrigation project, he suggests, was built up by progressive additions, each generation contributing a certain number of canals and reservoirs, using decentralized labour techniques (coordinated only at the village level). He concludes that when these works are carried out in their essentials at the village level, as with the system of Qanats in Iran, despotism does not necessarily result. Henri Goblot, *"Dans E'ancien Iran, Les Techniques de L'eau et la Grande Histoire,"* in Annual ESC, May-June, 1963. However, I believe, Goblot's studies of Iranian Qanats are somewhat limited and selective. While his description fits the characteristics of Qanats in the north part of Iran, it cannot be applied to southern part of the country. Especially, in the state of Yazd, the Qanats are massive and it is virtually impossible to construct the projects by simply relying only on local initiatives and generational contributions.

[5]For a thorough and systematic analysis of the Asiatic Mode of Production in general and Oriental Despotism in Iran in particular see Mohammad Amjad, *The Origin of Iranian Revolution,* working dissertation in the Department of Political Science, University of California, Riverside.

Iranian property relations were also despotic. According to Katozian, large-scale ownership of land existed but the landlord's share of central power was negligible. Katozian adds, "his claim was not bounded within an aristocratic tradition as in the West and his landed property could not always pass down to his descendents. Furthermore, large areas of cultivated lands were owned and administered by the state(khaleseh), or converted to the property of an Islamic institution of charitable wealth endowment" (Katozian, 1974:22).

While the Asiatic system in Iran contributed to rapid proliferation of villages, which in turn contained population growth and attached the peasantry to the land, its political ramifications eventually created a state of terror, and the use of arbitrary power undermined open thinking and entrepreneurship as the major preconditions for economic development. In a sense, the stagnant level of productivity became the Achilles heel of those who were resistant to change in the Iranian villages as population growth continued to suffocate the economy.

The gradual penetration of a market economy into the villages further contributed to the breakdown of the agrarian system and ushered in a socio-political crisis. The introduction of this new economic dimension to the antiquated agrarian system eroded the non-property land relations characterized by the Asiatic system. Using Marx's terms, this new dimension was stronger than a heavy artillery that could batter down the Chinese Walls.

The major consequence of this rapid socio-economic breakdown was a further lag in the economic productivity of the agricultural sector. According to both the Iranian census and Khamesi, the agricultural sector was extremely stagnant. This is evidenced by decline in per capita agricultural production during 1935-1961 (F. Khamesi, 1969:21). More detailed information for various years is presented in table 3.4.

The decline in agricultural output in the countryside had a devastating effect on the socio-economic life of large masses of cultivators, namely sharecroppers and khushnesheen. Many khushnesheen remained on the verge of starvation and some of them rushed to the cities. The conditions for a full-fledged agrarian revolution were now ready.

The land reform, which was essentially a political reform rather than an economic one, attempted to settle the land crisis once and for all. It aimed at the total institutionalization of political unrest. In this effort, the masterminds of reform put the strategic emphasis on the introduction of modern capitalist relations into the countryside. The concrete realization of this was the institutionalization of private property and of the hegemonic role of money and market relations.

Thus, the major Iranian villages prior to land reform can be characterized as follows: (1) Many villages remained overpopulated but still locked within the constraints of traditional land holdings; (2) There

60

Table 3.4

Index of Agricultural Production (AP) and Per Capita Agricultural Production (PCAP) in Iran: 1935-1961
(1952-1954 = 100)

YEAR	AP	PCAP
1935-1937	85	118
1937-1958	117	106
1958-1959	119	108
1959-1960	123	106
1960-1961	118	96

Source: Farhad Khamsi, 1969; p. 21.
Iranian National Census, 1956, 1966.

was a growing impoverishment among the lower rural classes because of the decline in agricultural output, and the escape of rural surplus to the main urban centers of absentee landlords; (3) Because of extreme poverty due to the breakdown of the agrarian system, the social conditions necessary for a genuine peasant revolt were in existence; (4) The beginning of a massive rural exodus; and (5) Active presence of a money economy in the agrarian system. With these factors in mind, we can now turn our attention to to the land reform itself and evaluate the extent to which it achieved its political and economic goals. This subject will be the topic of the next chapter.

CHAPTER IV

CLASS AND LAND RELATIONS IN RURAL SOCIETY AFTER LAND REFORM: RURAL PUSH AND MIGRATION

Land reform was an integral part of the Shah's White Revolution. The White Revolution, known also as a bloodless reform, itself was a comprehensive policy drafted and formulated by the Shah's top officials and U.S. experts in Kennedy's administration. The reform was initiated (superimposed) from above and the intention was to bring major change and modification in the organization and structure of the existing trouble-ridden traditional rural system.

Land reform, the foundation of the White Revolution, was implemented in January 1962. Its main goal was to redistribute arable lands among the lower rural classes who had cultivation rights under the old land tenure system (nasakh). This group of landless peasants was distinct from the khushnesheen in that they had "nasakh," that is, the landlord was obliged to provide the nasakh holders a piece of land on a regular basis.

Those nasakh holders who received land from the state were in turn obliged to pay annual installments to the representative of the state in the local villages. In this sense, the state became an intermediate link between the landlords and the sharecroppers for the legalization of land ownership, which had been jeopardized by the breakdown of reciprocal obligations. Approximately 1.5 million khushnesheen, however, were excluded entirely from the benefits of land reform, because land reform was drafted only for those peasants who had the right to cultivation (nasakh).

On the other hand, a number of landlords were excluded entirely from the law of land distribution and were permitted to keep their lands. Those who had orchards, tea plantations, and capitalist commercial type farms were allowed to keep their lands. This is a clear example that in land reform the state did not tamper with commercial agriculture; it acts only to keep the lid on traditional peasant agriculture. Additionally, each landlord whose land was cultivated in the traditional way was allowed to keep a six dang village for his own. A dang refers to one sixth share of any property.

62

A six dang village represented a medium size village with a sufficient number of cultivators, between 20 and 40, and adequate farming lands and water. Those villages that were below these standards were considered five dang or less.

This exemption from land reform was very beneficial to the landlord because he could choose a dang from his most prosperous villages and as a result he was in a position to control six villages (one dang for each village) at once. In many instances his past authority remained intact. Also the landlords could find legal loopholes to enlarge land property by transferring his land ownership to his relatives and dependents (especially in the second stage of reform).

The land reform was composed of four stages. In the first stage, which is considered the most radical part, 13,904 villages out of 48,500 villages were included in the reform. Among them, about 10,119 villages were less than an average six dang village property. Katozian estimated that only 15 percent of all existing villages were selected for land distribution. Furthermore, he claims that only 15 percent of all eligible cultivators of land received some land. Other writers on land reform have also arrived at similar figures (E. Hooglund, 1982:59-62). Thus, it is clear that the land reform format was not comprehensive enough to block all the possible loopholes which benefitted the landlords.

Ironically some landlords hurt themselves financially in the reform, due to their past tax evasion. Under Article 2 of the first phase of land reform, the price of land was determined by the Department of Agriculture. The price was calculated based on the amount of taxes paid by the landlords in the pre-land reform era. Many landlords, however, cheated on taxes by misrepresenting the true value of their property. The state took advantage of the situation and used it against its creators--the landlords. In those instances, the peasants who received lands became the main beneficiaries.

Those cultivators who were recognized to be eligible for land had to participate in the locally state-run cooperatives in order to possess the land. The program was mandatory for those peasants who received land in the first stage of land reform. The alleged intention of these cooperatives was to bring more autonomy and power to the peasants, so that they could run their affairs without a landlord's interference. In a sense, it was a rural institution erected to undermine the traditional basis of the landlord's authority.

The intended and latent functions of this policy, however, were to promote and extend the state's power into the countryside while providing a modern rural infrastructure necessary for the survival of small peasants after the departure of landlords. Given the traditional autonomy of local villages vis-a-vis the state and given the fact that the state had little say in the production process, the establishment of rural cooperatives should be understood as the first systematic effort in Iran's history to extend the state's hands to the very details of the organization of production in the agrarian society. Put in more simple language, it was an effort to establish capitalist relations of production in the countryside. The following officially announced functions of cooperatives demonstrate such an intention: 1. Operations concerned with production, exchange, storage, transport, and sale of the members' agricultural products. 2. The provision of agricultural implements and machinery, pesticides, and fertilizers. 3. The provision of primary necessities, such as food-stuffs, fuel, clothing, and household utensils. 4. The purchase of the agricultural products, or its storages and sale. 5. The giving of loans to members to tide them over the period until they sold their crops, and to provide what they needed for the cultivation of their crops, and, where necessary, sums for the improvement of the means of production, and loans on easy terms with low interest rates especially to members who had incurred debts at high rates of interest. 6. To accept deposits for members and to obtain credit (Lambton, 1969:293).

Using Robert Merton's language, the installed village cooperatives were supposed to be the "functional equivalent" of the traditional networks of support which existed among landlords, mobasher, kadkhoda, gavaband and others. Cooperatives were also responsible for integrating the local village economy with the regional and national socioeconomic structure. If the cooperative could manage to fulfill all these functions thoroughly, with no doubt the state of agriculture in Iran could have ben improved. As we will see shortly, for a number of reasons they fell short in meeting their officially announced objectives.

By the end of this phase of reform (February 1966), the state bought 2,883 full six dang and 10,038 less-than 6 dang villages. All of these villages were distributed among the qualified peasants. The peasants' total payment for the first installment added up to 178,190,260 tomans(at that time one toman was equivalent to one-seventh of a Dollar), and the overall state's debts to landlords amounted to 649,240,741 tomans. According to Lambton, more than 431,740 peasant families received land (Lambton, 1969:121).

It is obvious that the land reform is not limited only to the redistribution of land. It also covers other important rural issues considered critical to the rural economy. Generally, a comprehensive land reform deals with the following problems: 1)redistribution of land ownership; 2) land tenure reform(changes in policy regarding temporary leases and rental arrangements); 3) land consolidation, collectivization or rearrangement of private holdings or some combination of the three; 4) settlement, development of new agricultural lands or access to underutilized areas (J. D. Montgomery, 1984:4).

The second stage of land reform was implemented to address the remaining issues. It contained a number of supplementary articles formulated to facilitate the emergence of rural capitalist social relations among the cultivators and the landlords. Acts opened up four possibilities for the remaining villages: 1) to lease to customary tenants for thirty years at a fixed rent equivalent to the average of their net income for three previous years before the first stage of January 1962 every five years the landlords could renegotiate the rent with his tenants; 2) to sell the village and land directly to cultivators (the price of the landlord's property was assessed by the land reform agency); 3) to establish private cooperation with peasants receiving their share according to the tradition of the "five inputs" rules, which were locally decided on the share value of land-water-seeds-labor-ploughing cows (kheesh or joft);[1] 4) to divide the land with the tenants on the basis of former division of crops; the tenants received two-fifth of the land handed down by the landlords (Khamsi, 1969:24, Katozian, 1974:228). This stage of reform, like the first stage, did not benefit the conditions of khushnesheen at all. The combined effects of the first and second stage of reform are presented in table 4.1.

As this table shows, the total number of peasants who were affected by the reform is about 2,178 thousands. There are writers, however, that have estimated below two million. For example, Hooglund argues that all phases of land reform together benefitted only 1,938,728 individuals-which is about 92 percent of all nasakh holders in 1962 (E. Hooglund, 1982:72). The third stage of land reform dealt with the provisions for farming in the form of privately owned agricultural cooperatives. In many ways these were the extension of provisions of the second phase of the reform. Finally, the fourth stage of land reform, which was designed to fill the empty spots left by three stages, was ended prematurely by the November 1967 and the land reform was officially announced completed in 1970.

Overall, less than 10 percent of the villages affected received any land, and the villages affected accounted for 60-70 percent of the total. Grand total of perhaps 14-17 percent of Iran's peasants were made into new landlords-no more than 750,000 individuals. As we will see in the next section, the unintended consequences of land reform for the organization and the structure of villages were more powerful than its

---

[1] The system of the distribution of agricultural products amongst various beneficiaries of rural groups in Iran is called "sahmbaree." In this system there are five major elements of production: 1. land, 2. water, 3. labour, 4. seeds, 5. ploughing cows, and other primitive means of production. The agricultural products are distributed according to these inputs made by either the cultivators or the land lords. Usually, the landlord takes 2/5 of the products if he provides the peasants only the land. Other elements take up the remaining 3/5 of the products. Of course there is some regional variations across the nation over the laws of "five inputs."

The Size of Various Groups Affected by the First and Second Stage of Land Reform in Iran

Peasant who became owners	786,715	+
Peasants who became leaseholders	1,223,968	+
Peasants who became shareholders	153,111	+
Total	2,163,794	
Peasants who sold their customary rights	14,187	+
Total number of peasants who were affected by the first and second stages of the land reform	2,177,981	
Number of people who were affected by the first stage of land reform	621,501	+
Number of people who were affected by the second stage of land reform	1,556,480	+
Total	2,177,981	
Landlords who were engaged in farming exempted from land reform	725,535	
Mechanized villages exempted from land reform	1,277	
Orchards exempted from reform		

Source: 1. M. Katozian, Land Reform in Iran, JPS, 1974.
2. Bank Markazee, Annual Report, 1973-67.

intentional objectives of turning the peasant into a truly new-independent-entrepreneurial landlord. After all, it was a "white" revolution which lacked the courage and guts to confront and challenge the social basis of the landlords, most of whom were in the cabinet during the reform (even Arsanjani, who was the practitioner and bulldozer of reform and was known for his radical-socialist tendency, had an aristocratic background and possessed a large amount of land). These contradictions, inconsistencies and shortcoming in the program had a series of consequences for rural crisis and migration.

The Consequences of Land Reform: Deepening Rural Crisis

The land reform in Iran was primarily a state-sponsored initiative designed to control and divert the growing internal crisis in the rural economy. More specifically, the majority of impoverished rural residents did not have any voice in the shape and the structure of reform. It was purely a case of "change" from above. As a result, the bureaucrats and large landholders were able to manipulate the reform in the direction of their own interests. In fact, the total number of peasants who received some lands was a very small portion of landless rural dwellers. Overall, only between 740,000 and 787,000 peasants became land owners.

Similarly, other valuable resources (e.g., distribution of credit and machinery) indicate that the state was not sufficiently autonomous from the landed interests to act in the interest of the class as a whole. Rather, it allowed itself to become only an administrator or legitimator of value extracted by landlords. In fact, many large landholders, such as the Alam family, were part of either the cabinet or the royal family during the reform.

The land reform was partly formed in response to changes that profoundly affected the overall international community. The growing expansion of capitalist social relations at the global level necessitated some fundamental changes in the backward regions of the developing countries. In a sense, the land reform was a political intervention to alleviate the disruptive consequences of a socio-economic collision which was taking place between the traditional forces and the forces of capital arriving from "without."

As we will see, the reform, however, distorted the socio-economic fabric of rural society without destroying it altogether. It undermined and shook the old and despotic rural structure without ever replacing it with a modern capitalist structure. In fact, the failure of land reform instead led to the "break up" of the rural system, unleashing the previously attached-to-land residents migrate to the city. This is evidenced by the processes of land concentration and unequal distribution of credit in the rural society.

Land Concentration and Rural Push

The official intention of reform was to distribute the arable land more evenly among the rural residents. In practice, the results were quite different. Instead of an egalitarian land distribution, *the level of land concentration increased after the reform and fewer had access to more lands.*

Various studies have shown that the rate of rural-urban migration is closely proportional to the level of land concentration. For example, P. Shaw in his study of 16 Latin American nations effectively demonstrated that there is a strong relationship between the rate of land concentration in Latifundia and the rate of rural-urban migration. Griffin (1976), Guess (1979), and Karush (1979) have also arrived at a similar conclusion in latin American and Asian cases of rural-urban migration.

In the case of Iran we should notice that the growing increase in the concentration of land has occurred after a large number of rural residents had already left the countryside. Wei might assume that if those who left the countryside had remained in their place, the level of unevenness of land distribution would have been much greater (usually those who leave are predominantly poor or landless peasants). The available data quite satisfactorily substantiate the argument.

In 1972, after the completion of land reform, the situation of land distribution was as follows. 1. More than 11 million rural residents (approximately 62 percent of the entire rural population) had access to 38 percent of all agricultural land. The size of landholdings was between 1 to 10 hectares and land distribution was highly fragmented among small land owners. 2. More than 4 million rural residents (23 percent of rural population) were completely landless. 3. Less than 12 percent of rural population (2.01 million residents) monopolized more than 50 percent of all agricultural land (the land size varied between 10 to 100 hectares). 4. The remaining agricultural land (12 percent) belonged to only 7000 households or 36,000 individuals (size of land was larger than 100 hectares). 5. All small farms (1-10 hectares) produced 58 percent of all gross agricultural products, 23 percent of which was consumed in the market. In contrast, the large farms (10-110 hectares) contributed 42 percent of agricultural gross products, 77 percent of which was consumed in the market (extracted from the Statistical Center Iran, 1974).

In a number of case studies conducted by Iranian scholars, the Shaw's hypothesis of migration and land distribution in Latin America was reconfirmed. In 1974, 90 percent of all rural migrants from the province of Hammadan mentioned landlessness as the primary cause of their migration (Hommayoon Rafeye, 1974). Similarly in the province of Chahar Mohal, 62 percent of all rural migrants were composed of

landless khushnesheen. However, it was reported, albeit with less intensity and magnitude, that small farmers who had some lands also
migrated to cities. As we will see in the next section, inadequate support systems (e.g., lack of credit)coupled with pressure imposed by
large landholders, could also squeeze the small land owner out of business. The study effectively demonstrated a strong and positive relation
between the level of landlessness and rural migration (K. Khusravi,
1976).

The most recent study on the pattern of land concentration and
migration, conducted by Mohammad Hemmasi in the province of Fars,
replicated the findings for 16 villages with population of 12,000. It was
found that 1. approximately 88 percent of all migrants were landless
khushnesheen. In villages which were classified as having a high level
of migration, the khushnesheen comprised a greater percentage of
migrants. 2. On the average, 57 percent of all migrants mentioned "job
hunting" as the main reason for their migration. The impact of this factor on migration was greater in those villages which had a greater level
of rural out-migration. The relation between migration and occupational
structure of migrants is presented for three different types of village in
1979 in table 4.2.

In a study conducted in 1983 among the rural migrants who were
working in an automobile factory known as Iran Nacional (or Iran
Khoudrow) in Tehran city, the author found that more than 60 percent
of workers named landlessness as the primary cause of their migration.
There were 49 migrants whom I interviewed within that year.

At the macro level, a national agricultural census conducted in
1974 also reproduced the same pattern of land relations found in previous case studies of landlessness and migration. According to the
author's calculation, the level of land concentration indeed increased.
Although, the size of farming land enlarged after the reform (about 5
million hectares of arable lands), the volume of landlessness increased
substantially.

As table 4.3 shows, during 1960-1974, the number of small landholders and landless (those who had 5 hectares or less) increased from
1,221,180 to 2,111,541 households. This means that more than 890,000
poor peasant households were added during this period. Similarly,
despite their numeric increase, the average size of their farming land
decreased by 0.07 hectares per household. In case of large landholders
(5 hectares or more), their average farming land increased by 13,15 hectares per household, while their percentage of the population decreased
from 36.9 percent to 29.46 percent. This diminishing group, however,

Table 4.2

The Composition of Rural Migrants Based on Occupational Structure and Intensity of Migration in Villages Prior to Migration in 18 Selected Villages in the Province of Fars: 1979

Levels of rural out migration	Khushnesheen	Farmers	Students	Housewives	Total
HIGH	93.2	6.1	0.0	0.0	100.0
MEDIUM	87.2	3.0	8.0	1.3	100.0
LOW	78.5	13.0	0.0	8.4	100.0
TOTAL	88.1	6.1	0.0	8.4	100.0

Source: Mohammad Hemmasi; Bar-ra-see' Angee-zeh-ha Va Pe-ya-mad-haye moha-je-rat-haye Roos-ta-ee-yane' Be Shaher Dar Oastane' Fars. Shiraz University, Iran, 1979.

increased their share from 79 to 85 percent of all arable lands during this period, and the trend might have continued in subsequent years.[2]

Two major trends can be found in land relations before and after the land reform which stand in sharp contradiction with the alleged intentions of reform. 1. The number of lower classes who had little or no land increased, their share of all arable lands decreased, and their average land size also decreased. 2. The situation for the upper class residents was completely reverse. Their relative population size decreased while their share of land ownership increased, which meant greater disparity and contradiction between lower and upper rural classes at the level of land ownership.

What is critical to the understanding of rural push and land concentration is that the aformentioned two tendencies in land relations are strongly associated with the type of technology used in agricultural production. The small farm tends to be labor intensive and relies heavily on household labor, whereas the large landholders rely on labor saving technology.[3] This can be substantiated by the fact that the large landholders often depend upon the wage laborers. In a recent study conducted by the Plan and Budget Organization in 1984, it was found that when approximately 100,000 hectares of land are being transformed from traditional cultivation of wheat to fully mechanized cultivation, close to 60,000 agricultural laborers will be out of work.

From these analyses one may draw the conclusion that the reform actually widened rural inequality at the level of land distribution, it encouraged the use of more labor saving technology among the large landholders, and it deteriorated the overall life standard of a growing number of poor peasants. As we will see in the next section, even some of the small landholders who received some lands in reform were economically forced to give up their property and sell them to large landholders. Due to the lack of institutional, political, and financial supports, not only khushnesheen but also small landholders who were the beneficiary of reform could not maintain an attaching socio-economic life in the countryside. An examination of the structure of institutional support and credit systems will reveal the underlying mechanism of

[2]During 1966-1976 it has been estimated that more than 1.9 million rural residents moved to the urban centers (M. Alizadeh, 1984).

[3]The landless and small farmers(less than five hectares) had rarely employed wage labourers. The wage labourers comprised only 4.4 percent of the labour force in such holdings. In contrast, the cultivators who had more than five hectares of land rarely relied on the family type labour. This tendency is strongly felt among large landholders. It has been found that those who had 100 hectares or more land heavily relied on wage labour. The family type labour constituted only 8.9 percent of the labour force in such holdings. Source: (1) Statistical Center of Iran: The Second Stage of Agriculture Census, 1974; (2) H. Zendehdel, *The Structure of Labour Force in the Agricultural Sector of Iran*, Plan and Budget Organization, the Division of Manpower, 1983 (in Persian).

Table 4.3

Patterns of Land Distribution Among Lower and Upper Rural Classes Based on Households and Land Size in Iran: 1960–1974

Year	No. Households	%	Farm Land Total in Hectares	%	Ave. Hectares/ Household
	(Rural residents having less than 5 hectares of land or completely landless)				
1974	2,111,541	70.54	3,139,992	15	2.53
	(Rural residents that have more than 5 hectares of land)				
1974	881,876	29.46	13,980,791	85	44.68
	(Rural residents having less than 5 hectares of land or completely landless)				
1960	1,221,180	63.1	2,124,611	19	2.60
	(Rural residents that have more than 5 hectares of land)				
1960	712,983	36.9	9,231,563	79	31.53
Changes '60–'74	1,059,447	lower class (+7.36%) upper class (–7.36%)	5,060,907	lower class (–9%) (+9%)	lower class (–0.07) (+13.15)

Source: Adopted and calculated based on: Sar–sho–ma–ree Keshavar–ze, Ve–zarate Keshavar–se; 1960, 1974.

land concentration and migration in the post reform era.

State Funding and Institutional Support: Rural Push

Besides land concentration, the structure of state-sponsored fundings has a great influence on the pattern of rural unemployment, economic success, and standard of living via migration.

The institutional vehicle that was created to distribute credit and financial resources among the rural residents was the cooperative. These local entities, connected by national networks to the state's apparatus, were the immediate and locally based institutions designed to serve the basic interests of poor peasants who received lands after the implementation of reform. The available data demonstrate that the poor peasants were badly damaged due to the failure of cooperatives. The funds were divided among the rural classes quite unequally and the large landholders again were the main beneficiaries.

The cooperatives, installed as the functional equivalence of traditional patron-client system of support, could not fulfill their prescribed functions for the newly landeds peasants for a number of reasons.[4]

The cooperatives were mostly run by official bureaucrats who had inadequate knowledge about village life. Likewise, there was a lack of mutual understanding between the members of cooperatives and the state's representatives in those cooperatives. The newly landed peasantry often found themselves unable to present their grievances and needs to the officials. It would be unreasonable to expect peasants to participate in a quasi-democratic arrangement when yesterday the only mode of conduct was total obedience and submission to the lord. In addition, the existing red tape in cooperatives and the notorious bureaucracy were just impossible obstacles for the illiterate peasants to overcome.

The major factors that contributed to the poor performance of small independent farmers were the combined effects of unequal distribution of rural infrastructural resources and the unfamiliarity of new landed peasants with self-regulated environments. As will be

---

[4]Beside cooperatives, a number of agricultural **corporations** emerged after the land reform. Overall, they absorbed 32,506 members in 85 units and were given close to 41 million dollars by the state in 1976. The members had to give up their land title and to buy the corporation share instead. In many ways, the overall performance of corporations was quite similar to that of agribusiness. However, because of their relatively small magnitude vis-a-vis agribusiness and small-landholding, I shall not analyze their dynamism and structure further in this work. Instead, the focus will be on the behaviour of agri-business that had tremendous impact on rural employment anmd productivity. Overall, there were 89 corporations throughout the country in 1976. 813 villages were incorporated in these corporations and embraced nearly 320,509 hectares of arable land.

demonstrated, the cooperatives enchanced this growing structural incompatibility by allocating a great percentage of funds in projects that directly benefitted the wealthy residents of rural society.

It has been estimated that each member of the large landed bourgeoisie received on the average 80 thousands tomans from the state in the year 1976. In contrast, the small farmers obtained on the average only 200 tomans. The ratio of unequal distribution of government-sponsored funds is about 400 to 1 (80,000/200= 400). As a result, many newly landed small peasants were forced to search out new alternative lines of fundings. In many cases they had to borrow money from the local money lenders. According to the Office of Regional Studies in Iran, 32 percent of the 339 cases studied obtained money from non-government agencies at an interest rate of 25 percent or higher (A. Ashraf, 1971).[5]

Various studies show that policies which neglect the small farm sector tend to widen income disparity, sharpen social tension in rural areas and little assist the masses of the rural population. In a situation of population pressure and widespread unemployment, small farms have the considerable social virtue of providing more employment per unit area than large farms.

The economic bankruptcy of small farmers after the reform, as it will be empirically demonstrated, was one of the major factors that enhanced social inequality manifested in rising unemployment and income inequality. In the year 1970, it was found that a great percentage of rural residents had to work part-time, less than 24 hours per week. Although there is some variation across different regions, the general picture of under-employment in rural society was quite recognizeable. For example, in the province of Hammadan about 60 percent of male rural residents said they worked less than 24 hours per week (A. Majeedee, 1975). Similarly, in the year 1976, the overall rate of unemployment among rural residents was high, 13 percent among males and 22 percent among females (National Census of Iran, 1976). Nobody knows what the exact rate of unemployment and under-employment would have been if no rural-urban migration had taken place during this period, but certainly, given the great volume of rural-urban migration during that period, it would have been more than 60 percent in rural areas. The rate of under-employment in various regions

[5]There are many contextual variables that have conditioned and promoted the asymetrical distribution of agricultural funds. On one hand the large landholders effectively manipulated the state through familial-kinship ties and patron-client reciprocal networks that they always had within the state bureaucracy. On the other hand Iranian peasants could not effectively relate themselves to the state apparatus. Most of peasants were illiterate and had difficulties to participate in a historically scary and unfamiliar state. That is to say, the language of the state in solving the peasants' problems in most cases was drastically different from the one employed by the peasants in expressing their financial needs.

of Iran for both male and female is shown in table 4.4.

As far as income inequality was concerned, the practical outcomes of cooperatives proved that the state was unable to promote social harmony at the level of income distribution. This is evidenced by the rise of the Gini-index, a quantitative measure of income distribution and income inequality, in the later years. The index showed that except for the years 1970, 1972, and 1973, which are associated with oil boom in the Middle East, the rural society witnessed a growing rise of income inequality. Similarly, the measures of the "lowest 40 percent share" and the measure of the "top 20 percent share" showed a pattern of income

Table 4.4

Percentage of Rural Residents Who Worked Less Than 24 Hours per Week in Various Iranian Provinces: 1970

Province	% male	% female
Hamadan	59.4	30.0
Chahar Mohal	35.1	2.1
Isfehan	36.4	1.9
Khorasan	24.7	8.7
Mazaandaran	22.2	5.2
Kehkeeloyeh	13.8	N/A
Gillan	9.4	14.3
East Azarbayejan	9.4	14.3
Blochestan	6.8	8.2
Kermanshah	7.5	16.7

Adopted from the Statistical Center of Iran

Notation: In the year 1974, it has been reported by the head of the Organization of Budget and Planning that 40 percent of 3.5 million economically active population in the rural areas worked less than 24 hours per week. Abdol Majeed Majeedee, Dor Na-ma-ye Egh-te-sa-dee Va Ejtema-ee Iran, 1975 (in Persian).

distribution amongst various rural groupings. These two measures, of income inequality and Gini-index, are calculated for 1968-1979 and presented in table 4.5. They demonstrate the growing income inequality as it reached its peak in the year of revolution, 1979.

The root of this growing social inequality appears to be the structural imperfection found in the system of state's fundings at two levels

Table 4.5

Pattern of Income Distribution in Rural Areas of Iran in Various Years: 1968-1979

Year	Gini Index	The Lowest 40% Share	The Top 20% Share
1968	0.4014	16.9	46.4
1969	0.4071	16.6	46.7
1970	0.3904	17.4	45.4
1971	0.4008	17.1	46.5
1972	0.3979	17.2	46.7
1973	**0.3749	**18.0	**44.7
1974	0.4123	16.1	47.5
1975	0.3936	17.0	45.0
1976	0.4541	14.5	51.0
1977	0.4497	14.9	51.0
1978	0.4395	14.5	50.0
1979	0.4651	12.7	52.1

Sources:
1. Indicators of Income Distribution in Iran, The Organization of Budget and Planning, 1983.
2. The Pattern of Income Distribution in Rural and Urban Regions in Iran; Hameed Sohrabee, et al., The Organization of Budget and Planning, 1981. p. 13 (in Persian).
3. Nata-ye-je Amar-ge-re' Az Boud-jeh Khan-var-ha-ye Roos-ta-ee, The Statistical Center of Iran, 1980.

**Notation: For a few years that income inequality declined one can hypothesize that the decline could have been caused by a better performance of urban economy so that the rural poor could manage to leave the countryside toward the cities. That is, the systematic migration of poor peasants has caused income to become more equal among the remaining rural residents. In fact, in the year 1973, a sharp decline in income inequality is associated with the huge influx of petro-dollars into the economy.

in which the large landholders became the prime beneficiaries. First, the large landholders began to introduce a great magnitude of capital-intensive technology to their agricultural land. The landlords were often able to purchase equipment very cheaply with government credits. Many studies indicate the use of capital- intensive technology paves the way for a further increase of income inequality as it increases its users' income in the short run (C. Chase-Dunn, 1980:720). This took the form of extensive use of fertilizers and heavy machinery in the subsequent years, most of which are considered not strategically suitable for arid lands. The overall changes in the use of modern technology on farm lands are presented for the post land reform period 1963-1974 in table 4.6.

Furthermore, as the state subsidized the price of wheat and bread in the market for the urban consumers, the price of these strategical items declined below their true value in a "free" market. This policy in

Table 4.6

The Application of Technological Inputs to Iranian Agriculture During 1950-1974

| Year | Fertilizers (100 metric tons) | | | Tractors (100 units) |
	Nitrogenous	Potash	Phosphates	
1950	1.0	1.0	---	---
1963	73.0	18.0	86.2	---
1964	77.0	23.0	93.0	---
1965	127.0	17.0	111.0	11.3
1966	155.0	20.0	150.0	16.0
1967	330.0	13.0	280.0	17.0
1968	460.0	19.0	289.0	20.0
1969	490.0	20.0	300.0	20.0
1970	652.0	42.7	283.0	21.0
1971	1072.9	47.3	669.3	21.0
1972	1238.0	86.5	778.0	23.0
1973	1940.8	240.0	1333.4	106.0
1974	2485.7	250.0	1775.0	500.0

Source:
1. Food and Agricultural Organization, FAO Production Year Book.
2. The Statistical Center of Iran, Nata-ye-je Amar-ge-re-e Kesha-var-zee-e, Mar-ha-leh-e Dovvom Saar-shou-ma-ree-e Kesha-var-zee, 1974.

conjunction with the subsequent massive importation of grain and rice from the U.S. badly discouraged small farming business during 1970-1980.

Secondly, at the political level, the easy and unfair access to low interest rate credit not only allowed the large landholders to increase their incomes substantially with the use of capital intensive technology, but also they were able effectively to minimize the possibilities of a peasant revolt in the countryside. In other words, as more labor-saving technology was used by the landlords, the less bargaining power peasants had; modern technology could replace and substitute for the peasants' labor.

A number of studies demonstrate that extensive use of labor on the farm land often enhances the desire of laborers to own and seize the land on which they have been working and sweating for a long period of time. When such a desire for permanent ownership assumes organizational character and a leading ideology, it can lead to revolutionary behaviour under "favourite" conditions (Geffery Paige, 1975). The land reform could have unintentionally contributed to the formation of a peasant revolution from below, as it partially challenged the absolute domination of traditional landlords and indirectly encouraged the previously docile peasants to defy landlords.

It is interesting to note that many landlords were quite aware of the non-desirable political consequences of the attachment of peasantry to the land. Traditionally, since landlords had to rely on the extensive use of labor in pre-reform periods, they often prevented the crystallization of revolutionary conditions by the periodic *redistribution of land amongst cultivators.* That was a primitive technique but an effective one to *alienate the laborers from the land.* However, the modern landlords, with the help of easy credit, could accomplish the same goal by replacing workers with tractors and other labor-saving technology.[6] The interconnected process of land concentration, unequal distribution of credit, extensive use of modern capital-intensive technology, and finally the bankruptcy and migration of small landholders and agricultural workers, is well captured by Katozian in the case of Dez Dam:

> In 1968 ... in the Dez Dam areas alone, 58 villages with a total of 50,000 acres of cultivable land were affected. The result of this policy for the peasant households was a little short of expropriation. They were compelled to sell their land at administrative prices needed for their debts to the state and the cost of housing accommodations built for their resettlement. The peasant households lost their lands, their income, their cultural and sociological entities, etc., by one

---

[6]However, one can argue that the introduction of modern technology to the rural sector (agricultural production) has shifted the locus of revolution from rural areas to urban regions.

stroke... fifty five thousand peasants fell victim to this policy in the Dez Dam area alone (Katozian, 1978:361).

At the production level, land reform also failed. Although the large landholders received substantial financial resources from the state at the cost of the small farms, they could not fill the agricultural production shortages created by the erosion of small farmers and population growth. In particular, the agribusiness enterprises performed quite inefficiently despite the state's generous assistance. In many instances, despite various financial insecurities experienced by the small farmers, overall they did a better job than their well-fed large landholder counterparts (F. Etemad-Moghadam, 1978).

The effects of these compounding variables were quite serious for the Iranian rural economy in general and for agricultural production in particular. During the post land reform period, instead of improvement, the level of agricultural productivity declined in the face of massive migration and rural population growth.

During 1973-1974, for example, the gap between agricultural supply and demand for the major agricultural products amounted to 2,067 million dollars (Annual Report and Balance Sheet, Central Bank, 1973-74). A look at agricultural production of major items clearly shows why there was such a shortage of farming commodities. Production of rice declined from 1.43 tons to 1.15 tons during 1975-1980. During the same period, the production of wheat declined from 5.57 million to 5.2 million tons. The figures for other agricultural items are presented at the level of production and the size of land under cultivation in table 4.7.

The situation of agriculture in post land reform becomes quite frightening as one compares the performance of this sector with the national economy. The overall contribution of agriculture to GNP (excluding oil revenue) declined from 36 percent to 15 percent during 1959-1976. However, if one adds the contribution of the oil sector to the economy, the contribution of agriculture becomes almost negligible. In fact, during the same period the contribution of agriculture and livestocks together contributed only 10.3 percent of Gross Domestic Products, while more than 34 percent of the nation's labor force was engaged in the primary sector. This declining trend in agricultural production continued in the subsequent years as well. By the year 1978, the total contribution of this sector amounted only to 9.6 percent of GDP. The relative contribution of each economic sector during 1975-1978 is presented in table 4.8.

What is critical to the understanding of irregular rural-urban migration in Iran is an understanding of why, despite generous financial support to large landholders and agribusiness, the level of productivity

Table 4.7
Areas and Production of Selected Agricultural Commodities in Iran: 1975–1980

	Area (1000 Hectares)						Production (1000 Tons)					
	1975	1976	1977	1978	1979	1980	1975	1976	1977	1978	1979	1980
1. Rice	462	460	460	315	300	300	1430	1566	1400	1280	1212	1150
2. Wheat	5993	5631	5000	5000	4550	4500	5570	6044	5517	5700	5000	5200
3. Barley	1532	1481	1350	1300	1200	1200	1438	1487	1230	1000	970	1000
4. Maize	30	35	40	43	42	42	65	40	55	60	57	57
5. Sugar Cane	9	9	11	15	20	20	940	800	1000	1700	1750	800
6. Potatoes	50	68	80	80	81	82	506	550	697	680	688	697
7. Millet	20	20	20	20	20	20	25	25	25	25	25	25
8. Sorghum	10	10	10	10	10	10	12	10	10	10	10	10
9. Soybeans	54	75	42	65	70	70	70	102	86	115	130	131
10. Ground Nuts	2	3	2	2	2	2	3	4	3	3	3	3
11. Cotton Seed	NA	NA	NA	NA	NA	NA	252	284	323	240	181	130
12. Sesame Seed	4	4	4	4	4	4	4	4	4	4	4	4
13. Tobacco	14	17	13	13	13	13	14	19	15	15	15	15
14. Tea	16	27	26	30	30	31	21	22	20	27	28	29
15. Cotton	NA	NA	NA	NA	NA	NA	139	153	173	129	97	70
16. Jute	2	2	2	2	2	2	2	2	2	2	2	2
17. Wool	18	16	16	17	16	16	10	9	9	10	9	9

Source: Compiled, prepared from the data found in Quarterly Bulletin of Statistics for Asia and the Pacific.
V. XI, no. 2 June 1981 – United Nations.

Table 4.8

Contribution of Various Economic Sectors to Gross Domestic Product in Iran at Constant Prices in 1975 During 1975-1978

Economic Sectors	1975-1976		1977-1978	
	Rials (billion)	% of GDP	Rials (billion)	%of GDP
1. Agriculture & Livestock	324	10.3	344.7	9.6
2. Manufacturing and Mining	364.2	11.6	418.1	11.6
3. Construction	141.6	4.5	202.3	5.7
4. Water and Electricity	30.0	0.9	33.4	0.9
5. Oil (Iranian Share)	1,264.5	40.2	1,440.4	40.0
6. Services	1,025.0	32.5	1,158.6	32.2
G.D.P.	3,149.3	100	3,697.5	100.0
G.N.P.	3,210.8	---	3,722.0	---

Source: 1. Quarterly Economic Review of Iran, Annual Supplement, 1978, p. 5.
2. Economic Trends of Iran, B.P.O., Tehran, Iran, 1978: p. 21-27.
3. Annual Report, Central Bank of Iran (various years).

Important Note: Agriculture and livestock are composed of farming, pastures, animal husbandry and hunting, fishery, and forestry. Thus, the contribution of farming and pasture to GDP is way below. It amounted to 187 billion rials in 1975 and 223.50 billion rials in 1978 at the constant price at the year 1975. The share of farming and pastures to the total GDP was only 6.4 percent in the year 1978.

declined. The equivalent agribusiness in many Latin American countries has done a better job in terms of productivity. Unfortunately, the available research has been unable to tackle the question in a satisfactory manner. Some writers, such as Katozian, rather mechanically dwell on the inflationary role of oil revenue on the overall economy. Others look more into the problem of scarcity of skilled workers and lack of water, and still others consider bad management as the cause of problems. These explanations are at best descriptive and do not touch the roots of the problem.

Here, it is not intended to arrive at a definitive answer to the enigma of agribusiness failure. In fact, a series of serious studies on this problem is a great need. However, it can be proposed that the use of heavy machinery such as tractors and similar agricultural equipment is often unable to increase the level of productivity in those farms that have a basic water problem. Many Iranian farms are characterized by the problem of aridity. Under these circumstances, use of machinery only replaces labor without making agriculture more productive. In the situation of aridity, the best strategy would be to use more fertilizers, better hybrid seeds, and heavy investment in an irrigation system. Unfortunately, Iranian agribusiness went just to the opposite extremes; putting the main emphasis on the use of tractors ultimately led to the displacement of agricultural laborers and therefore out-migration.[7] After all, as we observed in chapter 3, one of the main problems of Asian countries in general and of Iran in particular is the problem of water scarcity. Any program which aims at solving the problem of rural unemployment, low productivity, and land concentration via migration must confront the problem of land aridity.

In conclusion, the impact of land reform on the general socio-economic structure of rural society and its consequences for rural-urban migration can be summarized as follows: 1. Extension of the state apparatus to remote villages in the form of cooperatives and agri-businesses. 2. Greater political control over the peasants' movements. 3. Formation of market oriented and capitalistic enterprises in the form

---

[7]According to the extracted materials from the agricultural census the following characteristics of farming land were identified in 1974: (1) The size of all Iranian land amounted to 164,800,000 hectares. (2) Only 10 percent of all the nations's space was arable land. (3) Approximately, 35 percent of all arable land was subject to artificial irrigation, due to the overall water scarcity in the nation. (4) All arable land, whether it was artificially irrigated or not, was not used for cultivation; only 2,858,872 hectares of arable land, which was naturally watered by the rain (Zamine Daymee) were cultivated for the production of agricultural foods. (5) There were 68,647 farm machines, of which 37,518 were tractors. The ratio of land to machinery (all machineries including tractors) was quite low amounting to one agricultural machine for 138 hectares of land. The ratio for the use of tractors was one tractor for every 248 hectares of land. Unfortunately, this trend became worse in the subsequent years. In the year 1980, on the average, the ratio declined to one tractor for 150 hectares of cultivated lands.

80

of agribusiness and cooperatives with a distorted structure and consequently bad performances. 4. Curtailment of the growing peasant revolt by redistributing some land amongst sharecroppers. 5. Over all failure to increase the level of agricultural productivity in rural units in their diverse forms. 6. Growing unemployment and income inequality resulting from unequal distribution of state sponsored funds and resources. 7. Growing impoverishment of landless peasants, especially khushnesheen, and greater concentration of farming lands in the hands of the landed oligarchy who began to use labor saving technology. 8. Malfunctioning of cooperatives and destruction of traditional networks of support which existed historically in the Iranian villages.

From these findings and generalizations, it becomes clear that the cumulative effects of land concentration, population growth, decline of the small farmers, and the credit system paved the way for massive rural-urban migration. The next chapter will examine the characteristics of the main urban centers in relation to their capacity to absorb the influx of migrants who can no longer maintain a viable life in the countryside. This examination is crucial since it identifies the major contradiction and incompatibility between the influx of rural population and the urban economy.

CHAPTER V

URBAN INDUSTRIALIZATION: MIGRATION AND URBAN PULL

During 1966-1982, more than 6.2 million rural residents came to the cities. As was shown in chapter II, the author arrived at this figure by making a number of adjustments on the basis of an exhaustive list of the components of urban growth in Iran.[1] In previous chapters the major political and economic variables of rural push in migration were identified; in this chapter, an attempt will be made to examine the extent to which, and how, the urban centers in the process of "industrial" transformation responded to this great rural influx.

Many developed European nations in their processes of industrialization and urbanization responded to the rural influx rather smoothly and harmoniously.[2] That is, the process of urbanization which was triggered by a rapid rural exodus simultaneously coincided with the rapid process of industrialization. This was evidenced by a conspicuous growth in the industrial sector in general and in the manufacturing sector in particular. That does not exist in the contemporary developing countries. The urban economy in the process of industrialization is unable to harmoniously respond to the influx of migration. In many instances, the rural influx not only damages the socio-economic structure of the place of origin but also causes stagnation of the urban economy as well. The latter occurs when the already deteriorating urban economy must host a large and growing pool of poor, undernourished, and unemployed migrants. The growing crises in the urban sectors in the form of over-congestion, immobility of resources, shortages in social

---

[1]In chapter II, nine factors were identified as the causes of urban growth besides natural population growth of urban centers and rural-urban migration. As was indicated, the contribution of these nine variables is often confused with the contribution of rural-urban migration to urban growth. In my calculation of the volume of migration to urban centers, approximately 20 percent was deducted from the rural areas to the urban centers in order to eliminate the effects of confounding variables.

[2]The term "harmonious" may hide various problems which were associated with industrialization in Europe. F. Engels has very vividly demonstrated that how capitalist industrialization was associated with the rise of misery and poverty among English workers in Manchester and in other major English urban centers. However, when the magnitude of problems in Third World countries is compared with the situation of 19th century Europe; the term may not be misleading.

82

infrastructures (such as piped water, housing, electricity, health centers), and unemployment signify the disjunction between rural out-migration and urban development and planning.[3]

The critical question that will be addressed in this chapter is: *why is the urban economy unable to respond harmoniously to the waves of migration? What are the basic factors that work against the urban economy and cause its stagnation in terms of creating productive jobs in non-farm activities?*

To answer this important question one must start with the analysis of the conditions and peculiarities of the manufacturing sector in the urban economy.

The manufacturing sector is crucial to an urban economy. It is the heart of urban industrialization. The available data demonstrate that this sector has been quite stagnant over time in most of the developing countries, particularly Iran. In the area of job creation, the performance of this sector has been the worst. During 1966-1976, the share of urban employment in the manufacturing sector did not follow the traditional and natural pattern found in the experience of the 19th century developing countries. Instead, the relative contribution of this sector declined, to the surprise of conventional wisdom. In 1966, the manufacturing sector embraced 27.7 percent of all the labor force in the urban economy. At the time of industrial take-off, the share in comparison to European experience is not normal. In subsequent years the share decreased sharply to the figure of 21.5 percent in 1976--a complete reverse trend in the processes of industrialization.[4] To understand such a surprise, one

---

[3]Although the poverty is displaced in the space, it has assumed a more organized character in the form of *collective consumption*. People might starve to death in remote rural areas without ever having been recognized or seen by the "world", but when the same event happens in the urban centers it has certain political and social repercussions on the state's overall political legitimacy. Urban problems, unlike rural ones, are very *visible in the developing countries.* In this sense, collectivization of problems, especially in the areas related to the reproduction of labour power (collective consumption) pushes the state toward arriving at urgent and quick solutions; the demand made in the cities is heard more patiently and more carefully than the one in the rural areas. There is a growing theoretical literature on urban consumption and urban demand making. The overall work of Manuel Castells, *Urban Social Movement and the Struggle for Democracy: the Citizens' Movement in Madrid--1978;* Stuart Lowe, *Urban Social Movements: the City After Castells--1986;* F. Pickvance, *The State and Collective Consumption--1982;* Mark Gottdiener, *The Social Production of Urban Space--1985,* on these issues is highly illuminative.

[4]It is important to note that these figures are only calculated for the manufacturing sector in the *urban areas.* Thus, the overall participation of nation's labour force in the manufacturing sector, regardless of its location (rural versus urban), is quite low relative to the European countries at the time of their industrial take-off. In 1966, the manufacturing sector in both rural and urban regions embraced only 18.5 percent of the entire employed labour force. This rate remained quite constant during the subsequent years. In 1976, the percentage share of the manufacturing sector of the total labour force was only 18.9 per hundred.

should pay close attention to the characteristics of the manufacturing sector in Iran. Such an examination reveals why the urban pull has been weak in this country.

The Characteristics of the Manufacturing Sector

The behavior of the manufacturing sector in terms of employment generation capacity, use of technology, level of productivity, dependency on foreign technology, quality of the available pool of labor, and concentration and spatial distribution of industrial units has with no doubt a definite impact on the waves of rural migration. Changes in rate and composition of these essential variables modify, expand, constrain, and delimit the behavior of the manufacturing sector in absorbing the rural migrants in the urban industrial sector. In other words, changes in the value of these variables determine the extent of discrepancy between the process of urbanization and industrialization and thus the volume of irregular rural-urban migration. Let's first begin the examination of this sector at the level of technology.

Tendency Toward the Use of Capital Intensive Technology

The kind of technology used in the urban sector is one of the major determinants of labor demand and level of unemployment. The more investment allocated to the use of capital intensive technology (henceforth CIT), the more workers will be out of work. CIT refers to those kinds of relatively sophisticated machines that can replace the workers by the process of automation. Thus, there is a reverse relation between the use of CIT and the capacity of the urban economic sector to generate new employment. Of course, the impact of CIT on unemployment is different for various occupational groupings. Certainly unskilled labor is displaced but there is greater demand for technicians and other white collars job for which the rural migrants are often not qualified.

Likewise, the use of CIT has a sociological effect on the existing pattern of social stratification and class inequality. It has been found by a number of sociologists that use of CIT specifically in the developing countries in and of itself causes a greater level of income inequality among the urban inhabitants (Myrdal, 1968; Chase-Dunn, 1980).

The pattern of industrialization clearly shows that the manufacturing sector in Iran has increasingly been using CIT since the beginning of industrialization (during the White Revolution). This is evidenced by the increasing size of invested capital in the newly formed firms in manufacturing and mining sectors during 1966-1976. In 1966, on the average, each worker worked with 0.6 million rials of capital and machinery. The ratio of invested capital to workers increased drastically in the subsequent years and in the year 1976 it was 2.3 million rials per worker. A similar pattern was found for the volume of fixed capital formation during 1966-1976. In 1966, the share of one worker was 404 thousand rials. In 1976, the rate increased to 1886.7 thousand rials per worker (A. Khaza-ee, 1984:10-15).

It is also possible to observe the accuracy of the CIT hypothesis by a longitudinal study of annual investment and new-employment-creation in the mining and manufacturing sector (data on the manufacturing sector alone are terribly scarce since they are presented for mining and manufacturing activities combined). Again the previous pattern of CIT and employment was replicated.

As the data show in table 5.1, the rate of organic composition (ratio of investment to worker) increased quite systematically during 1966-1976. In 1965, the rate of organic composition equalled 9.2 units. That is, for every worker who was employed in the mining and manufacturing sector about 9.2 thousand rials worth of new capital, machinery, and equipment was invested. Two years later, the rate increased to 13 units and by the year 1976, it was about an alarming figure of 103.36 units. That is, in less than 11 years, there has been about 1000 percent growth in the ratio of organic composition. This exponential growth of organic composition is more conspicuous during and after the oil boom which began in 1972.

Critics may question the validity of the conclusion made about the CIT hypothesis since some of the growth in organic composition can be attributed to the growing inflation in the economy during 1965-1976. While the criticism is valid, the author's calculation shows that even if one controls for the effect of inflation, the data still substantiate the argument (because the rate of inflation was not too high during the period). In table 5.2 the necessary information is provided for the number of workers and the amount of investment at constant prices of 1974 for various years during 1959-1976.

As the table demonstrates the value of organic composition was 13.98 units in 1965. It increased rather smoothly in the subsequent years until 1973. From that year on, the growth rate of organic composition was accelerated so that by the year 1976 it was about 71 thousand rials of new investment per employed worker in the mining and manufacturing sector. Thus, during 1965-1976, the growth rate of organic composition for new investment at fixed prices was about 400 percent. The organic composition at both current and fixed prices is calculated for the entire labor force in the secondary sector for the corresponding

Table 5.2

Pattern of Investment and Employment in the Manufacturing and Mining Sectors of Iran at Constant Prices in 1974

Year	(1000) Employment in Manufacturing and Mining	(million R) Investment in Manufacturing and Mining (Constant price 1974)	(million R) The Ration of Organic Composition
1959	971	N/A	---
1960	967	N/A	---
1961	974	N/A	---
1962	1012	N/A	---
1963	1051	N/A	---
1964	1074	N/A	---
1965	1137	15,900	13.98
1966	1274	17,600	13.81
1967	1360	25,400	18.68
1968	1470	38,800	26.39
1969	1591	46,400	19.16
1970	1724	52,900	30.68
1971	1809	56,400	31.18
1972	1908	59,700	31.29
1973	*2035	*89,700	*44.08
1974	*2184	*89,600	*41.02
1975	*2141	*146,700	*68.52
1976	*2285	*162,100	*70.94

Source: Calculated Based on <u>The Economic Trends of Iran,</u> Fifth edition, The Budget and Plan Organization, Tehran, Iran, 1978.

* As the data show after the year 1973, a rapid growth in the use of capital intensive technology is associated with the influx of petro-dollars in the nation.

of jobs created by that investment, the organic composition would be much larger than what it would be otherwise. In fact, the rate of organic composition for one new worker was 144.3, 339.9, 686.6, and 713.3 thousand rials in the corresponding year of 1966, 1974, 1975, and 1976.

These findings show that various measures of capital/labor composition yield a uniform pattern of increasing use of CIT in the manufacturing sector of Iran. One dollar of investment, whether at current prices or not, generates less and less employment over time as the new investment increasingly become CIT.

As will be shown in the following pages this pattern of CIT-investment is more pronounced in the cities than in the villages. This in turn becomes the major drawback for the urban economy to absorb the rural migrants in productive activities. In fact, large scale urban-CIT has not only decreased employment opportunities for the migrants but also it has driven the urban labor intensive factories out of business. Furthermore, as the size of firm increases, more investment in the form of CIT will be allocated. So let's examine and specify the effect of CIT and investment in the manufacturing sector at the size of firm (large firm versus small firm) as well as at the regional level (rural versus urban). The most recent data tend to support the argument.

Size of the firm is a powerful predictor of the volume of investment and employment. In 1966, large manufacturing units embraced more than 57.4 percent of the gross fixed capital formation at the current prices. In 1974, the share drastically jumped into 96 percent of all fixed capital formation. However, this rapid increase of investment in large units is not followed by a corresponding and proportionate rise in the volume of employment. In fact, in 1976, the large manufacturing units embraced only 24.7 percent of all employed workers in the manufacturing sector.

Furthermore, it is interesting to note here that large scale manufacturing units tend to be more concentrated in the large cities. The available data strongly support the existing strong and positive association between size of the firm and size of the city in which the firm is located. In 1979, it was found that 35 percent of all large firms that had between 10 to 19 employees were concentrated in Tehran city. The firms that had between 20 to 49 employees amounted to 1,263 units throughout the nation, 36 percent of which were located in Tehran city. This relation is presented in table 5.4.

The share of Tehran city increased for the subsequent larger category and it was 50 percent for all manufacturing units which had 50 to 99 employees. This pattern was consistent for the last category where more than 50 percent of all manufacturing units which had 500 employees or more were located in Tehran city. Given the fact that

Table 5.4

Distribution of Large Firms Based on the Number of Employees and Location in Iran: 1979

Location	10-19	20-49	Number of Employees 50-99	100-499	500 or more
Throughout the Country	1,946	1,263	602	487	204
Tehran City	681	459	241	207	92
The Ratio of Concentration	35%	36%	40%	43%	45%

Source: Adopted and calculated based on the Statistical Center of Iran, Statistics of Large Industrial Units in 1979 (in Persian).

many large firms are CIT, this growing concentration would have certain drastic implications for the rural migrants in the large cities.

Additionally, the skewed distribution of investment in favour of large capital intensive units has indeed cut off the necessary financial resources to small size and labor intensive manufacturing units in the nation. As a result, many of these units were driven out of business. That is evidenced by the decline of employment. In 1966, the small scale units (having less than 10 employees) embraced 87.3 percent of all employment with access to only 42.6 percent of all capital fixed formation in the manufacturing sector. In 1976, the share of employment was 75.3 (10 percent decline), while its share of capital fixed formation was about 3.5 percent (39.1 percent decline).

While all small units were hurt financially and lost employees, the effects of low investment were more devastating to the urban units than to the rural ones. The small scale rural manufacturing units miraculously survived in spite of financial cut-backs. This differential impact is clearly critical for the rural migrants who are looking for employment niches in the small manufacturing units in the urban areas. In 1974, the small size urban units had access to only 2.2 percent of all fixed capital formation (11.1 percent reduction during 1966-1974), and generated only 28.5 percent of all employment in the manufacturing sector (about 15.8 percent decline in employment during 1966-1976). In contrast, the small rural units did a better job on employment in spite of financial constraint. While their access to fixed capital formation declined from 29.2 percent in 1966 to only 1.3 percent in 1974, their share of employment surprisingly increased from 43 percent in 1966 to 46.8 percent in 1974. If we assume that the distribution character of capital formation of year 1974 has remained the same for the year 1976 (since there is no data for 1976), based on figures presented in table 5.3, it is now clear that the share of one worker in large firms to capital formation is about 135,000 rials whereas the share of a worker in rural small units to capital formation is only 983 rials. That is rural units with same amount of capital formation will contain 135 workers as opposed to one worker in the large units.

In sum, the increasing use of CIT and heavy investment in large units has had devastating consequences for employment opportunities in the urban centers. Although the major capitalist and professional groups have benefitted from this trend, the harmonious economic development in general and employment opportunities for the rural migrants in particular were substantially mitigated. Under these conditions, the rural migrants often faced a great deal of difficulty in obtaining regular and productive jobs in the urban manufacturing sector. Critics may point out that the contribution of an economic sector should not be limited solely to employment criteria; it should also look into its contribution to GNP and the extent of its productivity since it may indirectly contribute

Table 5.3

Employment and Capital Formation in the Manufacturing and Mining Sectors Based on Size and Location in Iran During 1966-1976

Size and Region		1966			1974	
	Capital Formation	(million R) Capital	%		(million R) Capital	%
Large Manufacturing Units		5,771	57.4		54,571	96.5
Small Manufacturing Units in Urban Areas		1,347	13.4		1,230	2.2
Small Manufacturing Units in Rural Areas		2,932	29.2		770	1.3
Total		10,050	100		56,571	100

Size & Region		1966		1976	
	Employment	Employees	%	Employees	%
Large Manufacturing Units		160,862	12.7	403,767	24.7
Small Manufacturing Units in Urban Areas		353,208	44.3	485,326	28.5
Small Manufacturing Units in Rural Areas		544,700	43.0	82,966	46.8
Total		1,267,600	100.0	1,672,059	100.0

Source: 1) Ahmad Khaza-ee, The Peculiarities of Manufacturing Employment in Iran (1966-1976), The Plan and Budget Organization, Tehran, Iran, 1984 (in Persian). 2) Iranian National Census, 1966, 1976. 3) The Statistical Center of Iran, Amar Karghah-ha-he Bo zo-r-ge San-atee-e Iran, 1966, 1974.

Notation: The data used here, however do not distinguish between manufacturing and mining and manufacturing sector. Overall, as was indicated earlier, the available data on manufacturing sector is mixed with the mining sector.

to the growth of the economy as a whole, thereby indirectly benefitting the migrants. In the next section these questions will be confronted and it will be shown that the manufacturing sector has failed in this area of testing as well.

Productivity in the Manufacturing Sector

The manufacturing sector in Iran is heavily dependent upon foreign raw material and technology. Most of the large manufacturing factories are engaged in the assembly and packaging of semi-imported goods and commodities and their productivity level is quite low.[5] During 1973-1974. amongst six leading modern manufacturing branches, three industries had negative value added to the imported inputs. During the same period, the input-output analysis showed that petrochemical, chemical manufacturing, and transportation equipment had respectively negative value added of 7324, 15943, and 21,436 million rials (Soofi, 1983:52).

The value added of the manufacturing and mining sector at the national level follows more or less a similar pattern. The existing information show that the level of productivity in the secondary sector was not proportional to the increasing size of investment. During 1959-1967, the value added at the deflator rate of 1974 was stagnant and did not show any sign of growth in spite of heavy investment. Diagram 5.1 contains the figures of value added of the secondary sector. The value added, with some fluctuations, was about 62.3 billion rials in both 1959 and 1969. As the diagram demonstrates, the value added of the secondary sector recovered from its long stagnation and showed some signs of relief during 1968-1977. The value added increased from 65.4 billion rials in 1968 to 115.8 billion rials in 1977. In other words, in more than 18 years, during 1959-1977, the value added had about 85 percent growth at constant prices in 1974. In comparison to the high volume of investment, this slow growth is not very encouraging. In fact, just during 1965-1976, the growth rate of fixed capital formation at current prices was larger than 2149 percent (source:Central Bank of Iran-- various issues).[6]

It is important to know that during 1959-1976, the percentage growth rate of fixed capital formation at current prices for all three economic sectors was only 256 percent (in 1959 it was about 52.7 billion rials). From these discussions and empirical comparisons it becomes clear that the manufacturing sector is characterized by an

---

[5]For example in 1965, the share of consumer goods, capital goods, and intermediate goods and raw material of the total import were 27.1 percent, 27.2 percent, and 45.7 percent. In 1977, the share of intermediate goods and raw material increased to 54.2 percent of the total imports in the nation (Bank Markazee Iran, 1965, 1977).

[6]The total value of fixed capital formation in the mine and manufacturing sector amounted to 10.5 billion rials in 1965. The figure raised to 236.20 billion rials in 1976; 2300 percent increase in 11 years.

Value Added in Manufacturing and Mining at Deflator Prices in 1974

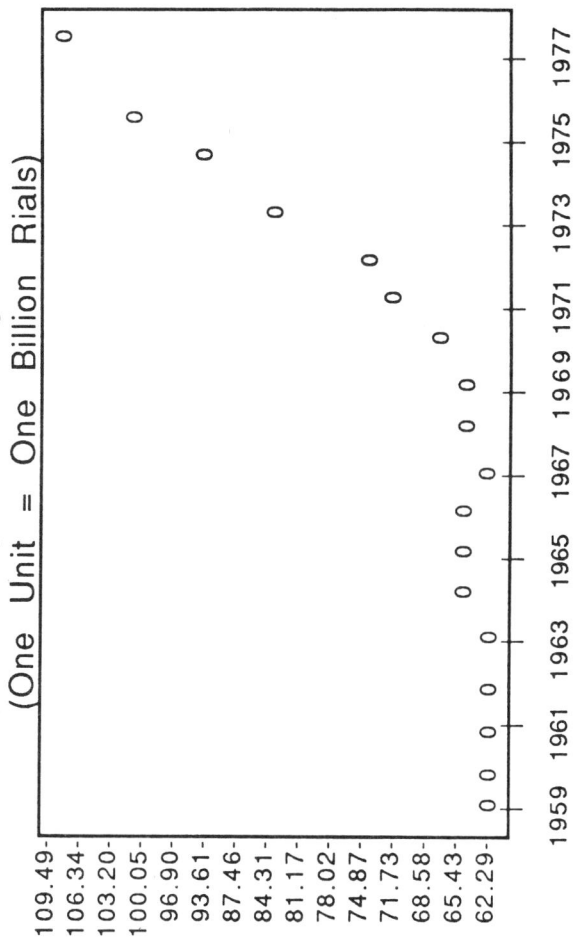

Diagram 5.1

(One Unit = One Billion Rials)

109.49-
106.34-
103.20-
100.05-
96.90-
93.61-
87.46-
84.31-
81.17-
78.02-
74.87-
71.73-
68.58-
65.43-
62.29-

1959 1961 1963 1965 1967 1969 1971 1973 1975 1977

Source: Economic Trends of Iran, Plan and Budget Organization, 5th Ed. 1978.

unusual combination of very low productivity, disproportionate and large volume of investment (but uneven in rural and urban regions), and very low employment creation capacity (especially in urban regions). By looking at this combination, one can conclude that the manufacturing sector has failed not only at the production level but also at the level of absorbing the rural migrants.

Why did the manufacturing sector fail at expanding both job opportunities and production capacities? The question is very critical to the problem of irregular rural-urban migration because as long as the urban manufacturing sector is unable to promote employment and as long as its performance causes income inequality and unemployment, it is expected that the rural migrants will turn into a social and economic liablity for the overall national economy during the process of industrialization.

There are many factors responsible for the discouraging character of the manufacturing sector. They are social, political, economic, as well as cultural. Although the subject is quite interesting and vital, it would be out of the scope of this study to list and analyze all the variables here. This study considers the nature of enclave industry, which is conditioned and sustained by the division of labor in the world system, as a crucial one.

The chief character of enclave industry is a lack of necessary inter- and intralinkages in the manufacturing sector. The leading industrial units are somewhat similar to isolated islands which have little interconnections or interactions with the national economy and its vital needs (e.g., uneven pattern of investment and capital formation in rural and urban regions, use of CIT during heavy unemployment and migration), but they are organically integrated into the economy of metropolitan nations. The outward character of the Iranian manufacturing sector and its heavy dependence on the economy of metropolitan nations appear to have limited the development of the necessary backward and forward linkages within the manufacturing sector as well as among all economic sectors within the nation. These linkages are essential for the growth and development of a self-sustaining economy which can simultaneously meet and confront foreign technological and economic shortages as well as urgent societal needs (unemployment, migration, agricultural revitalization, etc.).

In an input-output analysis carried out for the period of 1973-1974, the majority of leading industry met the criteria of enclave industry. The analysis showed that the industries in Iran had a low domestic backward linkage effect, high world forward linkage effects, and a high world backward linkage effect (Soofi, 1983:95-101). Often industries with the above characteristics cannot survive during major socio-economic changes and thereby create enormous problem of unemployment and economic deterioration in urban centers via migration. In a rare survey of major difficulties of leading industries in Iran it was found that the most advanced and thereby the most dependent industries had the greatest problems after the 1979 revolution. Many factories operated at low capacity and from the managers' point of view lack of foreign raw material, management, finance, personnel, and modern technology were responsible for the declining manufacturing units. The relation was best highlighted by the most advanced segment of the manufacturing sector, machine and metal equipment industries. This branch of the manufacturing sector was hurt the most after the outbreak of revolution. While it was operating at the highest level of production capacity among all the leading industries during peace time, its output drastically decreased during the revolutionary period.

As table 5.5 shows, this group of industries had the highest level of dependency on the world market. For example, in terms of dependency on foreign raw material, the score was 80 percent which is above all the percentage levels of dependency calculated for the remaining industries. While its production capacity under normal conditions in the pre-revolutionary period was the highest (86 precent), it moved in the opposite direction during the revolution. The rate of decrease in production capacity was one of the highest among the industries surveyed.

The correlation matrix also showed a similar tendency for all groups of industries in the survey. That is, the level of dependency is positively associated with the the level of production capacity during peace time ($r = +0.28$), and negatively associated with the level of reduction in production output during the revolutionary period ($r = -0.18$). The level of output capacity in peace time is in reverse relation with the level of reduction in output capacity in the revolutionary period ($r = -0.19$).

From these findings one may conclude that the level of irregular rural-urban migration has increased after the Iranian revolution. While part of it is due to the increase in the absolute size of migration in the recent years (between 120 to 180 thousands additional annual rural migrants after 1979), the declining urban pull, due to the restraining effects of dependency on productivity and employment, has undoubtedly played a major role. In fact, one of the major preoccupations of the present regime in Iran is the problem of unlimited influx of migrants to the cities with enclave industries that can no longer receive the necessary resources from the core nations. The growing disjunction between this labor supply and urban demand makes the problem of irregular migration more complicated.

Table 5.5

A Survey of Major Problems of Iran Industries After 1979 Revolution

Groups	% dependency on foreign raw material.	% production capacity of industrial unit under normal conditions.	% decrease in production. (Spring '80 relative to Spring '79)	Causes of low productivity in Spring '80 (from the view point of managers)			
				Raw Material	Finance	Mgmt. Personnel	Technical
Average: all units surveyed	72%	80%	28%	77%	59%	27%	50%	29%
Selected food industries	70%	88%	8%	42%	33%	17%	33%	33%
Machine & metal equip. industries	80%	86%	40%	100%	80%	36%	56%	28%
Construction industries	59%	79%	28%	100%	70%	30%	70%	25%
Textiles industries	71%	63%	28%	60%	50%	25%	40%	25%
Drug industries	75%	69%	11%	50%	42%	8%	33%	33%
Leather, paper & box industries	60%	66%	42%	50%	60%	20%	63%	25%

Source: A Survey of Problems and Difficulties in Iran's Industries, Bank Markazi Iran, Fall 1980 (in Persian) (The Department of Economic Statistics).

Changes in the Structure of Labor Market in the Manufacturing Sector

At a superficial level of analysis it is often assumed that the probability of finding a job in a region increases as the level of unemployment decreases. Although there is some empirical validity to this statement, it may not always be true for all situations, especially when there is an acute disjunction between the level of migrants' qualifications (education, work experience, skill, etc.) and the complexity of available jobs.

In many instances, the rural migrants come from underprivileged backgrounds with little education or training that can be used in the modern sector of the urban economy. In the case of Iran, the rate of illiteracy is very high and it is even higher in rural areas. In 1976, more than 82 percent of all 2.7 million employed agricultural workers were completely illiterate, unable to read or write. Another 8 percent could only read without being able to write. In other words, those who were completely literate (technical or general) comprised only 9.4 percent of all the employed agricultural population. The rate of illiteracy was even higher among the female rural dwellers. More than 96 percent of all females employed in agriculture were either illiterate or semi-illiterate (National Census, 1976).

While agricultural trainings, experiences, and backgrounds often become irrelevant to the work conditions of manufacturing activities in the cities, the relatively low level of automation of industries in Iran also undermines the absorptive capacity of urban industries. As Harry Braverman convincingly said, there is an increasing need to hire skilled workers in industry when the level of automation has not yet reached its peak. Although the use of CIT in Iranian industries has been the dominant trend, the level of automation in Iran lags far behind Europe. Such a level of automation requires a higher level of education, training, and skill that many illiterate Iranian rural migrants do not possess (Braverman, 1974:221-2).

In the fifth national planning (1973-1977), the Iranian manufacturing sector was confronted with a grave scarcity of skilled workers. During this period, for every needed 100 engineers there were only 55. The shortage of technicians amounted to 33 percent and it was worse in the case of semi-skilled and skilled blue collar workers. 31 workers were available for every 100 needed. Overall, the shortage of skilled workers, from engineers down to semi-skilled laborers, amounted to 613,000 empty positions.

The growing number of staff workers who are not immediately linked to the production line has also contributed to the rising difficulties associated with the absorption of rural migrants in the manufacturing sector. The existing information shows that the ratio of staff workers to manual workers is on the rise and that the trend is conspicuously pronounced in the large scale manufacturing units. As table 5.6 demonstrates, in 1966 for every 100 workers in the production line there were 9.5 workers who were employed as staff not directly linked to the actual processes of production; the number increased to 17.9 in 1976. A similar pattern was discovered in small scale manufacturing units, albeit with lighter growth. Given the fact that the staff workers usually enjoy skill and education, the increase in staff size is not in harmony with the needs and qualifications of rural migrants.

The scarcity and shortage of skilled laborers on one hand and the abundance of cheap, uneducated, and untrained rural workers on the other hand characterized the chief and yet paradoxical nature of the labor market in the manufacturing sector in Iran. This problem became more intolerable after 1979 when the intermingled national and foreign investment began to leave the country.

Table 5.6

Changes in the Ratio of Non-productive and Productive Workers in Iranian Industries Based on the Size of the Firms: 1966-1980

Size of unit	1966	1972	1976	1980
Small Units	1.6	2.2	N/A	N/A
Large Units	9.5	12.9	17.9	15.3

Source: Ahmad Khaza-ee, The Peculiarities of Manufacturing Employment in Iran (1966-1976); The Plan and Budget Organization, Tehran, Iran (in Persian), 1984, p. 50.

98

Foreign Investment

Various studies have empirically shown that foreign investment does not promote industrial development and urban employment in the long run in the developing countries (Chase-Dunn, 1980). It has been shown that the generated surplus and profit do not lead to capital accumulation but, rather, the major portion of it repatriates into the major core capitalist countries. Given the fact that foreign investment is usually CIT, the investment aggravates income inequality and unemployment in the Third World nations (A. Frank, 1969; Chase-Dunn, 1980).

In contrast, in 19th century developing countries, much of the development was due to the investment and reinvestment of profit extracted from the initial capital investment (one also needs to add the wealth of labor and natural resources accumulated during the colonial period). Such characteristics set the appropriate economic conditions for the expansion of urban economies where the rural migrants usually found jobs (the "discovery" of America alleviated the problem of rural migration and unemployment in the cities of Europe).

The available data for Latin American nations strongly support the argument (H. Magdoff, 1970). That is, the Latin American nations must pay 3 dollars of interest to foreign investors for every dollar invested, whereas in Europe and Canada it is one dollar of investment for one dollar of profit.

On the other hand, the foreign investors are not very much interested in solving the chronic problems of unemployment and economic stagnation. They are mostly concerned about their short run profit regardless of the pressing long term needs of the developing countries. For example, in the case of Mexico, foreign investment caused a major crisis in the economy of the border cities of Mexico. For a while, American businessmen invested a great deal of capital in the northern part of Mexico in hope of capturing the internal consumer market of Mexico and other Latin American nations. The investment caused a major population displacement and many rural dwellers decided to leave their villages to enjoy the the relatively high paying jobs created by the border economy. A few years later, US-Mexico border economic projects were pronounced dead due to the declining and quickly saturated internal consumer market in Latin America. As Fernandez put it, the failure of the US-Mexico border economy turned the border cities into "ghost towns." As capital left the regions, so did the jobs; instead poverty and prostitution replaced a once booming economy (Fernandez, 1977).

Although foreign investment was not a substantial part of capital formation in Iran (because of oil), it was effectively intermingled with the domestic economy and thus controlled it. The volume of capital, property, and assets that was smuggled out of the country after the revolution has been astronomical. It is estimated that the royal family and important cabinet members pulled 30 to 50 billion dollars out of the country; later, upper and upper middle class citizens who could not compromise with the Islamic government or did not want to live under Islamic laws also joined the crowd bringing their wealth and talent to Europe and the US. The volume of capital leakage has been so high that the freeze of 6 billion dollars of Iranian money in American banks in the Carter Administration loses its quantitative significance. These changes and leakages were disastrous to the urban economy and to poor migrants. In one word, *the volume of rapid economic decapitalization after the revolution has been immense.*

In sum, foreign investment is one of the factors critical to the absorbing capacity of the urban economy. Foreign investment in the major urban industrial units often promotes industrial instability and enhances income inequality, the consequences of which hit and affect the rural migrants the most. Although the great influx of foreign investment could enhance employment opportunities, there is no guarantee that such a trend would continue in the long run. Especially during major revolutionary structural change (e.g., Nicaragua, Philippine, Iran), investment leakages have an adverse effect on the capacity of the urban economy to contain the pushed out rural migrants in productive employment. Countries that are highly dependent on foreign investment and suffer from the scarcity of domestic capital will suffer the most.

Spatial Distribution of Industrial Activities

Factories and manufacturing activities have continuously gained more autonomy and independence from the variable conditions imposed by the Mother Nature. In contrast to manufacturing production, however, agricultural activities are inherently dependent upon the modes and cycles of nature. Despite the extraordinary human advancement in understanding, harnessing, and controlling the forces of nature since the industrial revolution, farming and related activities still continue to be subordinated to the boom and bust of seasonal cycles, natural barriers, drought, quality of soil, the amount of rain and light, and other factors. This differential subordination to nature in agricultural versus industrial activities has certain implications for the process of irregular rural-urban migration. What should farmers' villages do when the cycle of nature (specifically a long and cold winter) has stagnated agricultural activities?

This question is very critical to migratory movement in those societies such as Iran where the cycles of seasons are pronounced and distinct. For example, in those provinces such as Azarbiajan, Hamadan, and Zanjan in Iran which have long and cold winters, the level of agricultural activities is close to zero. On the average, farmers are unable to work more than 7 months in farming and related activities in each year. It has been reported that during winter time, between 750,000 to 1 million workers will be out of jobs (Agricultural Census, 1974). In 1976, about 99 percent of the 600,000 unemployed agricultural workers in rural areas were seasonally unemployed.

Naturally, during the stagnant seasons the farmers' income level will decline and they will be forced to search for new alternative sources of income. Employment in rural non-farm activities often generates the necessary income for the farmers in stagnant seasons. Without this alternative, the farmers will be forced to migrate to the cities either on a temporary or permanent basis. The non-farm employment can be considered as one of the most effective mechanisms to limit the effects of push factors caused by natural environment; it also indirectly helps the cities to develop as they are not overwhelmed by the non-absorbing flow of rural migrants. In addition, the non-farm activities diversify the employment structure of the rural economy. Various studies have shown that the diversification of occupational structure in an environment itself is one of the contributory factors that can mitigate the processes of labor displacement (Todaro, 1980).

Unfortunately, rural industrialization in general and non-farm employment in particular did not receive adequate attention from the Iranian government. As indicated earlier, during 1966-1976, the relative share of fixed capital formation in small scale manufacturing units in rural areas drastically decreased. The share to all fixed capital formation in the manufacturing sector in Iran was reduced from 29 percent in 1966 to only 1.3 percent in 1976 (see table 5.3 again). The significance of non-farming activities becomes more tangible as one pays attention to the spatial distribution of employment in the manufacturing sector. The rural manufacturing units generated 43 percent of all the manufacturing employment in 1966 and it increased, despite major cuts in funding, to 46.8 percent in 1976. In that year, about 783 thousand rural residents were employed in small scale rural manufacturing activities.

As the data reveal, despite declining resources in this important area of rural employment, non-farm activities, perhaps due to strong familial and kinship ties, have acted as a major resistor to rural push. One may surmise that without this growing employment opportunity, the present level of migration to the cities would have been even higher. Thus, those developing countries that suffer from the influx of rural migrants to the overcongested cities should promote non-farm activities by shifting the flow of investment to labor intensive industries in the rural areas. Since the manufacturing sector, on the average, requires a higher level of education than farming activities, investment

101

in this area also generates economic niches and opportunities for the rural pioneers who will otherwise flee to the cities.

In conclusion, the spatial pattern of investment, nature of technology, level of technological and economic dependency in the world system, productivity in the manufacturing sector, and the level of disjunction between the quality of labor supply and labor demand in the secondary sector, together set limits on the capacity of the vital sector of the urban economy to absorb the rural influx. When the constraining impact of these combined variables reaches its extreme, *one is tempted to use the concept of "urban push" instead of "urban pull"* to describe the limited employment opportunities in productive activities for the rural migrants. As we will see in the next chapter, in addition to economic and political variables, cultural and social structures also accompany and intensify this growing contradiction between migratory process and urban employment at certain historical junctures. Without this examination the study of irregular rural-urban migration would not be complete.

CHAPTER VI

THE RESIDUAL DETERMINANTS OF IRREGULAR MIGRATION: SOCIO-CULTURAL FACTORS OF RURAL PUSH AND URBAN PULL

In previous chapters the elements and causes of irregular rural-urban migration were identified at the level of the state and economic structure. More specifically, we looked into those politico-economic variables that *directly* shaped and determined the structure of income inequality and unemployment in rural and urban areas with two concrete outcomes: 1) disarticulation and decomposition of agrarian social structure in general and land relations in particular; 2) stagnation of the manufacturing sector and low employment multipliers in the urban center.

Often these two concrete outcomes, which are critical for the formation and expansion of irregular rural-urban migration, are reinforced and conditioned by social and cultural variables in the places of origin and destination. It is crucial to identify the relevant socio-cultural components of irregular migration in order to have a holistic understanding of the phenomenon under investigation. These non-economic variables (residual determinants), with differential impact, and in various historical conjunctures, complement the economic determinants of irregular migration.

Social Determinants of Irregular Migration

The social elements of irregular migration here refer specifically to the unequal distribution of social services in space. As the essential services become more and more unequally distributed with the urban centers surpassing the rural areas, rural dwellers are forced to move to cities in order to increase their access to such necessities. In other words, migration need not always be induced by changes in the structure of unemployment, poverty, and income inequality in rural and urban areas. Despite secure employment and adequate income, certain village dwellers (e.g., wealthy peasants, the small landholders) may choose to live in the large cities for easy access to major social services. As will be illustrated later, essential social services and amenities such as hospitals, doctors, schools and college, theaters, piped water and electricity are unevenly concentrated in a few major Iranian urban centers which may encourage migration of selective groups from the villages.

Given the existing congestion, unemployment, and excessive population concentration in the major urban areas which were described in chapter II, this non-economically induced migration has an adverse effect on the existing economic problems of unemployment, income inequality and growing concentration in the cities. In the following pages the spatial distribution and concentration of social amenities will be examined in the case of Iran; given the scarcity of data, the study will be limited to the capital city of Tehran.

One of the main characteristics of cities in Iran is that they increasingly swallow a disproportionate share of the nation's social services. This growing rural-urban disparity in terms of the distribution of fundamental and basic services has not only enhanced the growing tide of rural exodus but also has perpetuated the vicious cycle within which rural exodus and uneven distribution of services reinforce each other. Experience in the case of urbanization in Iran shows that once the reinforcing mechanism between migration and urban social services is formed it becomes very difficult to break the cycle. As a result, the pattern of the distribution of services in Iran is similar to an organism that has gained a huge head with a surprisingly weak and declining body. Tehran is metaphorically that head and the body is the remaining small cities and villages.

During 1960-1966, Tehran city alone embraced more than 68 percent of all university and college students, 46.1 percent of all large industrial units, 52.9 percent of all banking units, 57.9 percent of all available dentists, 42.6 percent of all hospital beds, 61.5 percent of all published newspapers and magazines, and 54.5 percent of all operating telephone receivers in the nation (Zonis, 1971; Kazemi, 1980). Given the rapid population growth in the city, the trend has unquestionably been aggravated in the subsequent years at the expense of other regions. Unfortunately, no systematic data on the distribution of services are available for Tehran city. However, there are reliable census data for the *county* of Tehran. Since Tehran city contains more than 85 to 90 percent of the population of the county, the available data can objectively portray the the service distribution for the subsequent years.

The available data reveal that the county has significantly and continuously increased its share of major social services. In 1975, the total number of doctors in the nation amounted to 11,760 persons from which more than 45 percent (5,299 doctors) resided in Tehran county.

Needless to say the best doctors usually live in Tehran city. According to the Ministry of Health, in 1974 all counties in Iran had shortages of doctors and the only one that had a surplus was the county of Tehran.[1] Similarly, the majority of dentists were concentrated in the same county. More than 50 percent of all 1,846 dentists visited their patients in Tehran county. The distribution of nurses and hospital beds was very skewed also. About 55 percent of all 5,145 nurses and about 42 percent of all 49,149 hospital beds were in Tehran county. Again the county had surplus and the remaining states had shortages of these social services. The most recent data after the revolution also show a similar pattern, albeit with some slight positive changes. In 1980 approximately 47 percent of all doctors, 52 percent of all dentists, 41 percent of all nurses, and 35 percent of all hospital beds were concentrated in the same county (M. Gheiyasee, 1982).

In terms of medical services, it was found that the village dwellers were badly neglected. In 1976, there were only *282 doctors, 30 dentists, and 869 nurses and midwives in all rural areas* (National Census, 1976); while there were 11,760 doctors, 1,846 dentists, and 5,145 nurses and midwives in Iran in 1975. In other words, the share of rural dwellers to the corresponding services was only 2 percent, 1.6 percent, and 17 percent in 1976. It must be remembered that despite the very low share of rural residents to medical services, rural residents comprised about 53.1 percent of the entire national population (there were 17,865 thousand rural dwellers in 1976). After the Iranian revolution, the state of inequality remains intact. During 1980-1981, about 6,348 doctors were employed by the Ministry of Health; only 19 percent of them provided their services to village dwellers. Similarly, out of 5,007 nurses and midwives who were employed by the Ministry of Health, only 134 of them were in rural areas (less than 3 percent). In terms of hospital beds, the rural dwellers were in their worst position; out of 57,374 beds only 553 units were found in rural areas (less than one percent) (Ministry of Health, 1980).

At the level of personal and social services such as school, recreational centers, there is a chronic scarcity of data for the examination of the spatial distribution of services in rural and urban places. However, one way to tackle the problem is to look at the behavior of overall employment in the service sector during the past three decades. Employment in the service sector may not be a perfect measure of real services rendered to rural and urban dwellers. For example, the service sector includes restaurants, which rural residents may not need. The service sector may also be the phony creation of market demands that provide marginal employment for the unemployed, like shoe-shine boys.

---

[1] One doctor for every 1000 people is considered standard for Iranian society. Anything above or below this standard-threshold is correspondingly considered as surplus or

Diagram 6.1
Patterns of Changes in the Distribution of Employment in Service Sector Based on Rural and Urban Regions 1956-1976

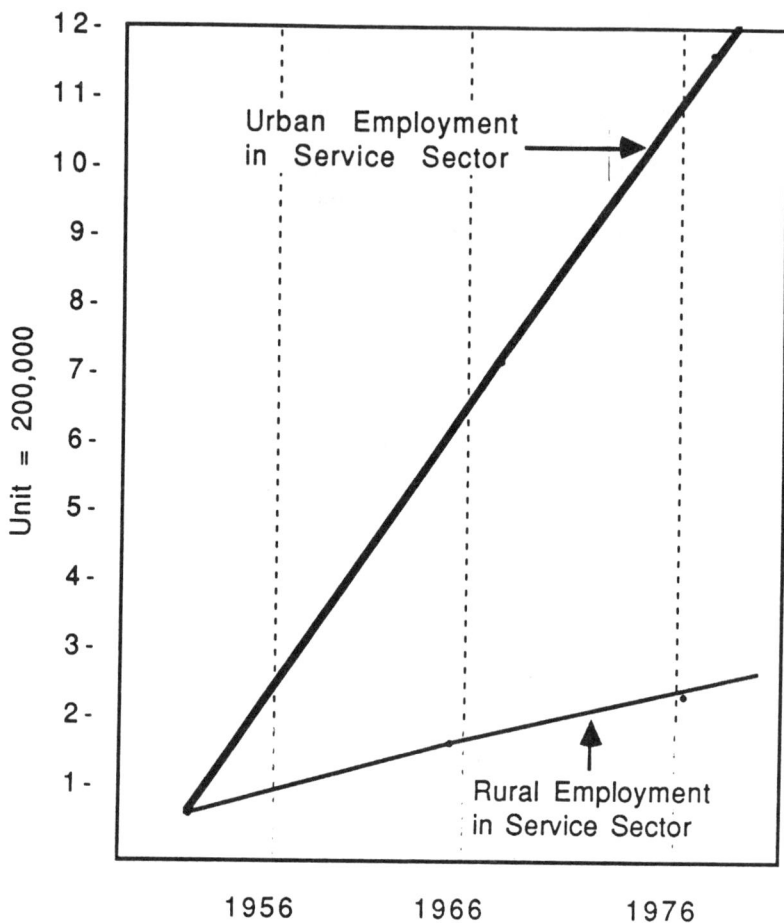

Source: National Iranian Census: 1956,1966,1976.

Given the existing measurement limitations, nonetheless measure of employment in the tertiary sector may provide some tangible impressions about the *aggregate* distribution of social services in rural and urban regions.

---

shortage of doctors.

Using this method, it becomes clear that while employment in services was at an earlier time distributed evenly it became increasingly skewed in favor of urban regions. Diagram 6.1 shows the trend during 1956-1976.

Prior to 1956, the distribution is perfectly even at the rural and urban levels. About 200,000 workers produced services for rural dwellers and about the same number offered their products to the urban residents. By 1966, the distribution had become uneven so that there were approximately 400,000 service employees in rural areas versus 1.5 million ones in the urban areas. And in 1976, the share of rural residents remained the same while for urban dwellers more than 2.6 million workers produced useful services for the urban dwellers.

Critics may point out that the declining share of rural residents to services is natural since more and more people reside in the cities and therefore they need more and more services. In other words, this apparent growing gap may not reflect the amount of services that rural people have actually received. Thus, to take into account the effect of regional population differences on the distribution of service, which has mainly been produced by rural-urban migration, one must compare the rural and urban per capita access to services. The necessary data are presented in table 6.1 and replicate the previous pattern of service mal-distribution.

Figures presented in column 5 and column 6 show the distribution of services in rural and urban areas after being adjusted for population changes during 1956-1976. The per capita share of rural residents to services remained quite stagnant for over 20 years at 3 service workers for every one hundred dwellers. The picture is quite different in urban places. Urban places embraced a greater level of employment in services in all three periods, and the gap between rural and urban places increased over time. In 1956, for every 100 urban residents, there were 8 urban residents active in the service sector. The ratio increased to 14 and 15 percent in the corresponding years of 1966 and 1976.[2]

As long as services continue to be disproportionately available to urban dwellers at the expense of rural residents, it is expected that excessive rural-urban migration will flourish regardless of unemployment and other obstacles in the cities. In other words, the unequal distribution of necessary services in space would have interactive effects on rural push and and urban pull, promoting the forces of economic

---

[2]In my interview with rural migrants both in Tehran-car-industries and squatter settlement, I found that poor health facilities in rural areas played an important role in bringing rural residents to Tehran city.

Table 6.1

Changes in the Distribution of Services in Rural and Urban Places During 1956–1976 in Iran

Subject:	(1)	(2)	(3)	(4)	(5)	(6)
	Rural pop.	Urban pop.	Employees in rural service sector	Employees in urban service sector	3/1	4/2
Year						
1956	13,001,000	5,954,000	353,055	454,914	0.03	0.08
1966	15,994,000	9,795,000	471,952	1,414,239	0.03	0.14
1976	17,865,000	15,797,000	485,495	2,371,388	0.03	0.15

Sources: Iranian National Census, 1956, 1966, 1976.

rural push and urban pull and thus irregular migration. Inadequate infrastructural services act as one of the major obstacles to rural industrialization by which the forces of rural push are significantly limited and constrained. Rural industrialization requires skilled workers, experienced technicians, and educated bureaucrats and managers, most of whom reside in the cities and show little interest in working in backward and underdeveloped areas. Although they are often paid better in rural areas than in the cities, they prefer to stay in the cities as they have guaranteed access to qualified doctors, hospitals and other crucial service necessities. Employed or unemployed rural residents may also migrate to the cities for similar services.

On the other hand, the maldistribution of services also sets limits on the economic absorptive capacity of the city-- namely urban unemployment and income inequality-- as it attracts more migration to the cities. The concentration of services in the major cities can act as a pull factor in migration while there is an absence of urban pull at the economic level, such as employment opportunities and higher income. In 1972, the agricultural census shows that the majority of migrants who were previously employed in the place of origin remained unemployed or economically inactive in the cities. Fifty nine percent of all migrants(rural and urban residents) who migrated to the Tehran city remained either as unemployed or economically inactive (children, housewife, elderly, etc.). The rate of unemployment for women, who usually have an active economic life in rural areas, was particularly high; more than 93 percent of all female migrants in Tehran city were either unemployed or economically inactive. In contrast, approximately 23 percent of male migrants were unemployed after their migration. More than 40 percent of all unemployed and economically inactive migrants were found in Tehran city during 1972-1973 (see table 6.2).[3]

From these findings in Iran, it can be projected that the maldistribution of services in terms of both quality and quantity, particularly health and education, is a strong motivating force which may stagnate the economy of rural and urban areas. Regardless of whether this impact is direct or indirect on the economic structure of employment and income level, it encourages the expansion and growth of irregular migration. It can be concluded that as long as the state in the developing countries in general and in Iran in particular formulate politically and regionally biased policies that aggravate the spatial maldistribution

---

[3]It is worth noting here that much of the non-industrial employment in Iranian cities can be viewed as a kind of desperate self-help job creating effort, in which rural migrants in cities, facing a very limited expansion of industrial jobs, are forced to settle for a variety of marginal odd jobs such as street vending and domestic services. These types of employment often are not fully reflected in the official records of employment statistics; and in fact they can be considered as one of the most conspicuous example of unemployment and underemployment in the cities.

109

The Structure of Employment & Unemployment Amongst Migrants After Migration in Tehran and Iran, 1972

Region	Subject Sex	Employed	Unemployed or Economically	Total	The Ratio of Economically Inactive to Total Pop.
Tehran City	Males & Females	713,441	1,028,714	1,742,155	59%
	Males	657,183	248,450	906,033	27%
	Females	56,258	779,864	836,122	93%
Iran	Males & Females	1,683,775	2,591,095	4,274,870	60%
Tehran (-----) Iran	Males & Females	42%	40%	41%	---

Sources: Calculated and adopted from:
1. Nata-ye-je Amar-Gee-ree Nee-ro-ye En-sa-nee Sahre-Tehran, 1972.
2. Nata-ye-je Amar-Gee-ree Nee-ro-ye En-saa-nee Ko-lle Keshpvar, 1973.

of necessary services, it is expected that rural-urban migration will continue to flourish in spite of growing unemployment and insufficient economic opportunities. This becomes more evidenced as one brings the demographic variables into consideration; they continuously depress the economic conditions in rural as well in urban places.

Demographic Determinants of Irregular Migration

In addition to social forces of irregular migration, the population factor is a major non-economic variable that has caused the excessive flow of irregular migration. It has enhanced rural push while it has limited the expansion of urban pull-- namely the urban economy.

Population growth in Iran as elsewhere is the result of the growing gap between death and birth rates. The death rate has continuously declined due the widespread use of modern medicine, while the birth rate does not show any sign of decline. Families in rural and urban areas continue to bear many children, many of whom now survive. This so called "demographic transition", in today's developing countries, shows *no sign of "transition"* to a new state of population stability that most of today's developed nations have experienced. One may interpret this persistent demographic gap as a classic example of *cultural sectivity* whereby the intrusion of modern technology and Western culture differentially effects different components of population parameters and thus promotes unevenness and contradictions.

There are many reasons for the persistence of a relatively high birth rate and pregnancy among the people of developing countries. However, given the overall economic stagnation in the developing countries, economic variables in conjunction with deep-seated religious values can be perceived as the major sources of the problem. That is to say, economic insecurity which is particularly created by the initial population growth, in turn becomes an active agent of population growth itself. Most of the lower stratum of rural and urban inhabitants are economically insecure and they combat the problem by having more children, who soon become an investment in the labor market. In other words, the likelihood of finding a job for the entire household (as the social unit) increases as the size of family, namely children, increases. This relation is reflected in the differential rate of population growth in rural and urban places. Since, on the average, there are more poor families in the rural areas than in the urban, the available statistics show that population growth in urban areas has been substantially below the rural population growth in spite of relatively inadequate social services mentioned before. For example, during 1972-1976, the net natural urban population growth (birth minus death) registered 24.2 per thousand vis-a-vis 34.9 per thousand in rural areas. The figure was 30.3 per thousand for the entire nation.

Additionally, the excessive rate of population growth in rural areas has a direct effect on the rate of natural urban population growth. First of all, the distinction between the effects of migration and natural increase may be blurred when, after the migrants' arrival they bear children who are counted as part of the natural increase rather than migration. Secondly, rural migrants tend to have higher fertility rates than their urban counterparts because they are disproportionately younger and fall in the most active reproductive age category and because they carry their rural reproductive values with them.

Diagram 6.2

The Distribution of In-Migration to Tehran City in Each
Specific Age-Group During 1971-1976

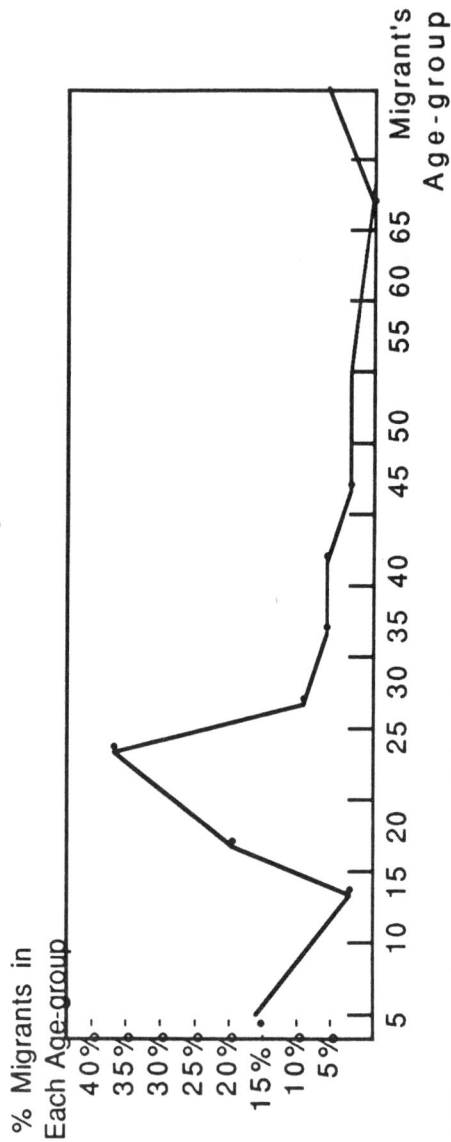

*Migrants refer to those individuals who were resided in Tehran in 1976 but were not
in Tehran in years prior to 1971.
Source: Data were calculated from Iran's 1976 census.

For example, the majority of migrants (about 70 percent) who settled in Tehran city during 1971-1976 were between 20 to 30 years of age. Diagram 6.2 demonstrates this relation visually; the data are presented for 13 age groupings.

In many developing countries including Iran, the rural population, with its relatively high fertility rate comprises more than 60 percent of the entire national population. Naturally, this rate of rural population growth should increase the overall rate of national population growth. With few exceptions, it has been found that the rate of national population growth is positively and strongly correlated with urbanization and the concentration of population in urban districts. Under constant conditions, the higher level of urban population growth would diminish the capacity of the urban sector to absorb the added population, most of whom have rural backgrounds. A comprehensive study conducted by the United Nations in 1,212 cities of developing countries in 1983 supported the argument and showed that for every one percent difference in the national growth rate of population there would be one percent in the urban growth rate (United Nations, 1983:M249). Similarly in Iran, the same pattern was discovered. As we saw in chapter 2, the regression coefficient became stronger after the year 1940 when the rural economy and its accompanying social organizations began to deteriorate.

As long as the rural and urban rates of unemployment and income inequality are low and as long as the urban economy is growing and expanding rapidly and as long as population growth in rural areas does not depress the overall functioning of the rural economy, a high level of urbanization (which means a high level of rural-urban migration) in and of itself should not always be considered a major problem in terms of rural push and urban pull. Population growth and rapid urbanization become problematic when the induced tides of rural migration cause growing income inequality, and high rates of unemployment in rural and urban centers.

It is now appropriate to examine the effects of those cultural variables on migration which increasingly accentuate the magnitude of rural push and depress the urban pull. With this examination it becomes clear how cultural variables condition, reinforce, and limit the economic, social, and demographic determinants of irregular rural-urban migration.

113

Cultural Determinants of Irregular Rural-Urban Migration

The decision to migrate is constrained by economic, social and cultural variables; each shapes and influences the other variables. Albeit a difficult task, a comprehensive analysis of any kind of social action should ideally include and consider not only socio-economic and demographic variables but should also pay close attention to the dynamism of transformation in symbolic systems in the processes of industrialization and integration in the world economy.

While migration, viewed as social action, is predominantly a calculated, conscious, and rational behavior performed by the individual migrants, it can be an irrational, destructive, and economically unproductive action when viewed from the macro level of the entire social structure. In other words, the effects of cultural transformation on the migratory process should be kept analytically separate at the micro and macro levels since the effects are different. At one level it promotes the short-term interest of the individual migrants and at another level it undermines the entire socio-economic foundation on which migrants live and procreate in the long term.

In what follows, attention will be paid to changes in the *value system* that have caused the stagnation of the urban economy, particularly the manufacturing sector, and hence low urban pull, unable to integrate the rural migrants in the city. Then, it will be argued that changes in the structure of traditional value systems among the rural residents, caused by the intrusion of Western culture and ideology, have promoted and encouraged migration, a great proportion of which has not been in the interest of rural society. That is, the act of migration has become a symbol of status and power in those villages whose residents' standards are now shaped by urban values.

It is necessary to answer two critical questions in order to understand how cultural change as an autonomous structure effects the volume and form of rural exodus: 1. How have the ideology of modernism and Westernism in general and consumerism in particular reduced the capacity of the productive urban sector to absorb the growing urban population? 2. How have these cultural factors in turn weakened the legitimacy of the traditional cultural pattern and encouraged rural-urban migration in the face of high urban unemployment?

1. Low Urban Pull and Modernization of Values

Accumulation of capital and continuous growth of investment in urban industries, holding other conditions constant, positively contribute to the growth and expansion of employment opportunities in the initial phase of capitalist industrialization. In the history of industrialization in today's developed countries, these conditions guaranteed the absorption of rural migrants in productive enterprises. But the causes of rapid expansion of urban sectors, particularly manufacturing, were not all economic and in fact the cultural factors and basic transformation of predominant values played a major role.

Max Weber became a pioneer among the masters of sociological thought, by paying great attention to the role of values, strong and passionate commitment, and deep-held beliefs in the study of social change in general and the rise of capitalism in particular. According to him, the very interplay of the emerging value system, in the form of the Protestant Ethics, with economic variables culminated in the rise of a new modern social structure-- modern capitalism-- which was unprecedented in its high level of production and growth. The nature of ideological, philosophical, and religious values expressed in the totality of superstructure is a powerful weapon capable of transforming the entire structure of an economic system.

According to Weber, the teachings of Luther and Calvin emphasized four principles among their disciples, which later brought about the most productive economic system known to humans. First, profit and acquisitiveness, beside reflecting one's success in the economic world, was also an indication of personal virtue. As long as wealth is accumulated through legitimate and legal means it should be seen as a sign of virtue and well-done religious duty. Second economic activities and work, beside maintaining human life in the earthly world, are ends in themselves inseparable from one's religious calling. Earthly economic activities are in fact preparation for the heavenly and otherworldly life. Third, a Protestant believer does not enjoy the "privilege" of repentance and atonement, possible in Catholicism, for past ungodly conduct, mistakes and sins. The absence of confession and a mediator between God and individual, including sacraments and a mystical union with God, created a psychologically intense state of inner loneliness in Protestant believers (in terms of whether the person will be saved or not) that could only be healed and overcome by rational, hard, and consistent work.[4]

---

[4] The author have to share a personal experience here with the reader. When Grace Von Tobel, a Protestant believer, was proof-reading the final draft of this manuscript, commented in the margin that her existential experiences and understanding of Protestant ethics do not correlate with the content of this third proposition.

Fourth, the believer was prohibited from an idle life and luxury consumption, and encouraged to delay worldly gratification. The earning of wealth should be combined with the avoidance of using this income for personal enjoyment. This last principle was an offshoot of the second principle, the heart or *summum bonum* of- Protestant doctrine, which emphasized pecuniary success and the earning of more and more money as an important indicator of salvation. Thus, according to Weber, religious commitment in intense and disciplined worldly activities, together with moral resistance to a consumerist life style, unprecedently unleashed the rapid expansion of productive forces in the European nation.

With no doubt, Weber was not all successful to eliminate other "rival hypotheses" of the rise of capitalism. Number of scholars such as Kurt Samuelsson, R. H. Tawney, Ephraim Fischoff, and Gabriel Kolko have effectively shown that while there is an empirical correlation between Protestantism and modern capitalist organization, the Protestant Ethics was not the exclusive cause (e.g., cases of capitalist development in predominantly Catholic and non-Christian nations). Irving M. Zeitlin also shows that Weber, in his reaction to the "ghost" of Marx, has exaggerated the role of ideas in social change in general and the Protestant Ethics in capitalism in particular. The author, like these writers, believes that the Weberian interpretation of history should be accepted tentatively with a critical eye to its limitation and its hidden ideological underpinnings.

Materialist writers, such as Marx, who stressed the role of material conditions in history, are not all blind to significant role of ideas in social change as Weber wants us to believe. For example while Marx highlighted in *Communist Manifesto* the importance of material conditions--such as the discovery of America, the rounding of the Cape, the East Indian and Chinese market, colonialization of America, trade with colonies--in the development of capitalism in the West. He maintained in his *Early Writings* and *Grundrisse* that once "revolutionary ideas and ideologies" penetrate the masses, they become "material force themselves." Second, "capitalism is 'ascetic' in that the actions of capitalists are based on self-renunciation and continued reinvestment of profits... Political economy, the science of wealth, is, therefore, at the same time, the science of renunciation, of privation and saving. Its true ideal is the 'ascetic' but 'usurious' miser and the 'ascetic' but 'productive' slave... The passion for wealth as such is a distinctive development, it is not natural, but historical" (A. Giddens, 1971:214-5).

These two giants, whose works in social science and philosophy are viewed by many contemporary scholars as antitheses to each other (for example see M. Zeitlin and his notion of Marx's ghost in the development of sociological theory), seem to agree on the existing *cybernetic relations* between economic development and value-directives expressed in the unique cultural and psychological make-up of a society.

As far as the study of irregular migration and urban pull is concerned, industrialization and Westernization of developing countries have in fact distorted the positive ingredients of the old culture and socialized the individuals to consumerist values now prevalent in the late 20th century developed nations. More specifically, these values have retarded the development of urban manufacturing sectors in which many rural migrants might find jobs. In the case of Iran, the retardation of manufacturing sectors, as we saw in Chapter 1 and 5, occurred despite fertile economic opportunities generated by the oil boom during 1972-1980.

Existing research in many developing countries shows that the necessary cultural muscles for rapid industrialization are conspicuously weak. The culture that has been transfused from the Western nations into the developing countries, particularly after the end of World War II, often encourages extensive consumerism and idleness, this is particularly true among the middle and upper classes, who have access to a disproportionate share of wealth and power and who are supposedly in charge of bringing entrepreneurship and productivity to the dynamic sectors of urban economy.

Western capitalist societies in their later stages of development have significantly deviated from their previous asceticism and adapted themselves to a new cultural orientation of capitalist-promoted consumerism, often necessitated by their recent systemic economic overproduction.[5] While extensive consumerism and recreational activities in the developed nations may temporary alleviate the problem of overproduction created by an insatiable international competition and expansionism, they have done little to assist the developing countries in overcoming their present state of socio-economic stagnation and rapid urbanization. The recent diffusion of Western cultural profiles and its selective acceptance in the developing countries have encouraged a premature luxurious life style which has diverted the necessary resources from investment in productive activities in general and in manufacturing activities in particular.

---

[5]In addition to economic conditions, consumerism and consumption of luxurious goods can also symbolize one's social status. That is, consumption of goods and luxurious commodities among affluent classes have been increasingly "transfunctionalized" from use value (e.g., function values) to sign value. Sometimes, this transfunctionalization mechanism reaches its full performance to the point that the mass cultural objects which have been derived from consumption of the good's function values, intertwines with ideologically fabricated connotation (e.g., Simulacrom). For an excellent review of this important problem see: Mark Gottdiener, "Hegemony and Mass Culture: A semitic Approach," AJS, Vol. 90, no. 5, (March 1984).

Portes' work on this subject is very illuminating. He describes the modern orientation as a dynamically self-seeking psychology, a conscious desire for benefits of life in advanced countries, and a willingness to acquire the necessary skills for attaining a similar life style. These characteristics, it should be added, are quite similar to McClelland's conception of Achievement Needs, which he sees so necessary for economic development (D. McClelland, 1963). However Portes argues that this attitude can spread throughout the population, without altering the permanent situation of underdevelopment (Portes, 1973).

A crucial difference between developed and underdeveloped economies is that, while increases in consumer demand tend to stimulate further growth in the former, they shrink opportunities which are so necessary for the development of the latter. The basic reason is that demand in a mature industrial economy tends to generate multiplier effects which, commencing with consumer-goods industries, promote demand and growth in other sectors of the economy; the latter sectors in turn revert to light industries, forming an upward spiral (Myrdal, 1968:1186; Hirshman, 1958).

In contrast, consumer demand, encouraged by the diffusion of Western culture and status values, tend to force an increase in imports in countries where the industrial plants are rudimentary or where an import substitution-oriented-industry is not backed by a diversified economic complex which already includes heavy industries. Depending on the situation, the misuse of resources can either occur directly by importing pre- or semi-fabricated manufacturing goods or indirectly by importing raw and semi-processed materials and basic machinery. In both cases, scarce foreign exchange is spent for immediate consumption, thus restricting investment in long run development (Portes, 1973; Furtado, 1964).

In addition to noting the direct and indirect effects of importation on the urban industrial economy one should also be sensitive to the role of multinationals in the developing countries. It has not infrequently been observed that these companies *force* countries and firms to import their products, through aid agreements, patents, inputs into commodities they are producing as well as through advertizing and promotion schemes. In such instances, one should enrich the sociological analysis of urban industrialization by incorporating the effects of the political economy of imperialism into the cultural interpretation of retarded industrialization in the developing countries.

The pattern of cultural change and its consequences for the particularly urban economy in Iran during 1960-1980 fits quite accurately Portes' description of cultural change in Latin America. The available data show that much of the investment resources in Iran was spent on unproductive and luxurious projects. During 1973-1978, according to Reza, the non-development spending amounted to nearly 95 billion

118

dollars, while oil revenue were only 90 million dollars (A. M. Reza, 1980:107). It has been estimated that the key items in the non-development account were: 1. Defense: 39 billion dollars, most of which were destroyed by the outbreak of the fierce Iran-Iraq war, departure of American military advisers during 1980-1981, and a shortage of military parts rendered by the breaking of diplomatic relations with the USA during the hostage crisis. 2. luxury housing and food imports amounted to 13.5 billion dollars. 3. Net additions to Pahlavi wealth amounted to 12.5 billion dollars and 4. SAVAK and other lesser items fill out the list (J. G. Scoville, 1984:2).

In sum, the diffusion of Western values, especially a consumerist orientation among the affluent classes, works to undermine the positive elements of traditional religion and culture which are essential for the mass mobilization of resources for an internally oriented socio-economic development. In this respect, industrialization within the cultural framework of Westernization often tends to spread new values in society that are inconsistent with those goals that are set for economic growth and full employment. These values, in conjunction with economic and social circumstances, particularly contributed to the rise of unemployment and overall economic stagnation in Iran.

This cultural argument does not, however, explain why people move to the cities; it only " explains" why the cities are not expanding economically. It is an explanation of what happens to the migrants when they get to the city. To examine the direct effects of cultural factors on irregular migration, we should focus on the changes in the rural value system as they "push" the rural dwellers toward the cities.

2. Rural Push and Cultural Demoralization of Rural Society

The majority of leading social thinkers in urban and modernization research have been preoccupied with a cultural dichotomy which presumably exists between village and city dwellers. It is not infrequently said that urban culture is superior to rural culture and that the latter will inevitably be transformed and dissolved into the former in the course of industrialization and modernization.

Redfield's conception of folk-urban society (1968), Simmel's description of metropolitan civilization and *blase* attitude, Wirth's theory of urbanism as a way of life, Durkheim's conceptualization of mechanical and organic solidarity, and more recently the whole Chicago tradition of urban sociology headed by Professor Park can be viewed as a number of systematic attempts to understand conceptually the qualitative differences between rural and urban culture. These writers have implicitly argued that rural culture in the long run will be assimilated to and subsumed under a historically more developed culture, namely an urban way of life and its associated symbolic system.

This conceptualization of rural and urban culture has contributed to the rise of an outlook that sees the different mode and form of social organizations as the actualization of evolutionary processes in time and space. Particularly, two giant historians, Spengler and Toynbee, pushed such an evolutionary bias to its ultimate logical conclusion by equating Western culture and civilization with that of urban culture (Spengler, 1928). From this vantage point, the dichotomy of rural and urban culture is isomorphic with the dichotomy of traditional/modern society.

Rather than going into a detailed evaluation of this cultural dichotomy from a critical point of view, it is more important to recognize the asymmetrical relation between rural and urban places. The pattern of irregular migration in developing countries is particularly formed by the cultural dominance of large cities over the villages. In many ways, this dominance has contributed to the weakening of traditional and communal culture in the villages in the rural areas. In many instances, the breakdown and demoralization of traditional culture, along with or independent of social and economic parameters mentioned before, have dissatisfied the rural dwellers, especially the younger ones with the old culture.

The relation of cultural dominance between cities and villages is primarily of two kinds. 1. The cultural prestige and high status associated with urban life from the view point of urban dwellers. 2. Inferiorization of rural residents rendered by the diffusion of urban culture; particularly through mass media. The author in his interviews during 1982-1984 with rural dwellers who had resided in Tehran city has the impression that rural dwellers respect any village residents who "made it" in the city. Any single success may encourage a new wave of migration especially among youngesters whose parents have no "eyes" to see many cases of failure such as poverty, long term unemployment, and crime among other migrants. Particularly, if the cost of migration has been high (due to the long distance journey), the younger migrants said they could not return and face their parents without some tangible evidence of material gains. The author will not contemplate how this situation of desperation could lead to various forms of crime and personal demoralization. Similarly, many city dwellers, especially if they are from large urban centers, stereotype villages dwellers in a pejorative form. This relation of power often enhances a sense of inferiority and low self-esteem among rural migrants.[6]

---

[6]In Persian language the term "*Dehat--ee*" is used to denote village dwellers. "Dehat" is a plural name and means "villages", and "ee" changes the meaning from "vil-

In 1982, an intensive interview with rural migrants in a squatter settlement in Tabriz city, located in the north-west of Iran, showed a strong sense of inferiority among the residents. The respondents, who were 325 female migrants from villages, were asked to express their opinion about "city women." It was found that more than 40 percent of the residents considered them as superior. Only 13.5 percent perceived no difference and only less than 1.7 percent believed that city woman is inferior, weak, and unable to face and solve tough problems of life. The same study also showed that the female migrants found their traditional clothes embarrassing to wear in public and in fact more than 80 percent of the respondents no longer used their village dress after arrival. More specific responses can be found in table 6.3 and table 6.4.

As these studies show, a majority of rural dwellers in Iran attribute more values and status to the urban way of life as they internalize and accept the inferiorizing definition of rural life from the the perspective of urban dwellers. It can be concluded that as long as urban culture continues to be the main source of power and prestige, it is to be expected that the indigenous communal culture in various forms will degenerate, lose its grips to hold village dwellers to the land, and thus encourage migration.

Table 6.4

Pattern of Changes in Behaviour Among Rural Migrants in Tabriz City, Iran

Do you still use and wear your village (traditional) clothes?		
	Total	Percent
YES	77	19.2
NO	325	80.8

Source: K. Housain Zadeh Daleer, The Tabriz Shanty Dwellers, Tabriz University, 1982.

lages" to "village-dwellers." When a city man or woman, especially the one from Tehran city, uses this phrase to call somebody in a verbal fight, it has very negative and pejorative connotation. It means irrationality, stupidity, untrustworthy, dirty, barbarian, and non-human.

Table 6.3

Attitudes of Migrant Women Towards City-born Women in Tabriz City, Iran

HOW DO YOU SEE URBAN WOMEN?

	Total	Percent
They are superior to us	136	40.0
We are envious about them	4	1.1
There is no difference	49	13.5
We do not like their manner	7	2.0
We see them as loose ladies	9	2.6
They are weak and cannot solve the tough problem of life	6	1.7
We are not migrants (from Tabriz)	26	7.6
I do not know them well	84	24.7
No answer	22	6.4

Source: K. Housain Zadeh Daleer, The Tabriz Shanty Dwellers, Tabriz University, 1982.

Conclusion

These chapters sought to demonstrate that the processes of irregular migration from the countryside to urban centers are interwoven with economic, social, demographic, and cultural factors. Each influences another while each has its own autonomous forces of migration. Although the economic variables- income differentials, unemployment rates in the places of origin and destination, industrial growth or retardation, land reform and land distribution-- play the essential role in displacing population from rural to urban places, it was shown that social, cultural, and demographic variables were also important factors in excessive and irregular migration in Iran.

More specifically, these structures were analyzed in both rural and urban areas to see how they intensified the overall forces of rural push on the one hand and drained cities power to absorb the migrants on the other hand.

To avoid the methodological trap of absolute relativism, which cannot delineate the analytical importance of one structure over another in an explanatory scheme, the state was introduced as an intervening factor to organize and systematize the complex interplay of various structural effects on the migratory process (e.g., role of the state in land distribution, in social service distribution, in promoting cultural dualism). In the case of Iran, given the overconcentration of power and wealth in the hands of the state during its history of oriental despotism, the structural effects of economic, social, demographic, and cultural variables on migration were overwhelmingly conditioned by the performance of government as a whole. Especially in economic and social realms, the effects of the state's policies have been detrimental.

Now it is time to treat the phenomenon of irregular rural-urban migration as an independent entity, to ask how this form of migration effects the entire social structure? The consequences of irregular migration for society are very diverse and cover many subjects. We will analyze only its most important aspects- housing crisis and squatter settlements. In the remaining chapters, the scope and form of the housing crisis in Iranian cities will be analyzed and it will be explained how migrants in various squatter settlements continue their struggle for shelter and survival.

CHAPTER VII

CONSEQUENCES OF IRREGULAR
RURAL-URBAN MIGRATION:
SQUATTER SETTLEMENTS

Irregular rural-urban migration has many effects on the places of origin and destination. While in some areas it might induce positive changes in society, the author believes that its primary effects are disruptive and deleterious to smooth and sustained socio-economic growth and development in today's developing countries. Particularly, the impacts of irregular rural-urban migration on the major urban centers have been very sever and multifarious, and the author substantiates this "belief" by closely looking at one of the most tragic problems of urban crisis--the squatter settlements.

Squatter settlements are very complex phenomena in the developing countries. They are primarily formed in response to the growing housing crisis which itself is triggered partly by the disruptive rural-urban migration and partly by the stagnation and maldistribution of the housing industry (see Chapter 8). Squatter settlements have many forms and therefore we need to define the term carefully.

What Is a Squatter Settlement?

There is little agreement as to an exact meaning or definition of the widely used term squatter settlement. The confusion arises from both a proliferation of labelings by commentators and from real variations in the internal composition of the phenomenon. The literature is filled with numerous labels that emphasize different conceptual approaches. A brief review of the literature on urban crisis in the developing countries very quickly reveals this problem.

John Turner coined the term autonomous urban settlements (Turner, 1960); various United Nations' writers have used the terms spontaneous, marginal, transitional, sub-integrated, provisional, non-planned, uncontrolled, and unconventional as interchangeable with the "squatter." Peter Lloyd, one of the leading authorities in urbanization in the Third World does not even offer a precise definition and reluctantly uses "slum", "squatter settlement", and "shantytown" interchangeably (Lloyd, 1979).

Various local names have further compounded this definitional chaos. In Mexico, squatter settlements are known as *Colonial Proletarias*. In Panama, Venezuela, Peru, Chile, Uruguay, Brazil, and Turkey, the corresponding terms of *Barriada Brujas, Ranchos, Barriadas, Callampas, Cantegriles, Javelas, and Gecekondu* respectively, have been used. In the popular press and journalistic reports it also is not infrequent to find *marginal settlements, clandestine urbanization, barrios of invasion, parachutists, phantom town, and favela* as the substitutes of squatter settlements.

In Iran, various local names are also used to denote the phenomenon of squatter settlement. *Zagheh, Tappeh, Goed, Hallabeeabad, Kappar, Alonack, Chador, Kooreh Paz Khaneh, Hasheh Nesheen, Mohaleh Koleeha* are used by both social scientists and common people to refer to the phenomenon. All of these local names express, however, a sense of poverty and destitution in the settlements.

The lack of clarity about the nature of squatter settlements is also a reflection of objective differences among the settlements. It must be born in mind that a squatter settlement is not a unitary phenomenon; that is the settlement is characterized by a *combination of a number of factors* whose outcome-profile varies from one squatter settlement to another. Basically, the critical characterizing components of a squatter settlement should be expressed in terms of access or lack of access to urban infrastructural facilities as well as to residential legal rights.

The characterizing variable of a squatter settlement should be conceptualized as spectrum with variable values in various time and places. In this way, one can categorize and distinguish diverse forms of squatter settlement. Probably John Turner was the first scholar who recognized the diversity and heterogeneity of settlements in various places of the developing countries and attempted to grapple conceptually with the definitional problem of squatter settlements. Although he did not offer a definitive definition, he generated a useful typology of squatter settlements.

According to him, squatter settlements' residents are in constant struggle to improve the quality of their residential places. He identified two groups of settlements. The first type of settlement is occupied by recently arrived migrants who have build their houses with extremely low quality materials, often called "bridgeheaders." Turner sees the formation of a squatter settlement as a process in which the quality of life and of housing are constantly improved by the residents. Therefore, in his eyes, as the bridgeheaders fortify their socio-economic position in the urban economy and improve their legal stand and tenure rights in the city, they increasingly improve the quality of their housing to the point that Turner calls the occupants "consolidators." In other words, a squatter settlement itself is a variable phenomenon subject to improvement and modification in the course of time.

On the other hand, C. Strokes, while echoing the developmentalism of Turner, believes that the attitudes and belief systems of the community are the critical variables, with or without which the transition from the bridgeheaders to consolidators may or may not take place. According to Strokes, there are really two kinds of settlements. The first one is filled with individuals who are delinquent, with no regard to progress and mobility--what he called the "slum of despair;" the other is made up of achievement-oriented residents who are optimistic about the future, work hard and believe that one day they will become legal middle class citizen themselves. He named this community the "slum of Hope," whose residents' characteristics are quite opposite to what is known as the "culture of poverty" (Strokes, 1962).

Neither Strokes nor Turner has been very sensitive to the macro structural variables of poverty and marginalization. Turner sees continuous progress and development in migrants' life conditions in the city and Strokes believes that the widespread problem of poverty and despair is really a problem of wrong attitude.

Probably the first person who made a systematic effort to arrive at a useful definition of squatter settlements in the relevant context of housing crisis is Charles Abrams. According to him, the main characterizing definition of squatter settlements revolves around the "forcible preemption of land by the landless and homeless people." The reinterpretation of Abrams' theoretical definition of squatter settlements thus rests on the mode of urban struggle towards the forced appropriation of privately owned land. The major ingredient of squatter settlement formation is its violation of basic tenets of capitalist property relations.

In a more careful study of the housing crisis in Iran, it is observed that there are many poor migrants as well as urban dwellers who live in rented or owned dwelling units in low income communities; using Abrams' conceptualization these people, despite their high level of poverty, cannot be considered as squatters. Kazemi in his study of poor migrants in Tehran city, argues that "most of these communities can be characterized as slums by common standards. They resemble the traditional core-city slumlord tenants found in many urban centers throughout the world" (F. Kazemi, 1980).

There are also other urban dwellers (migrants or not) who not only struggle against poverty on a daily basis but also have no stable residential place. The author, in his field work of urban poor in Tehran city in 1984, was overwhelmed by the sheer number of homeless people who "resided" in parks, streets, or under bridges, similar to skid row residents in large American or European cities (Bahr, 1973). Since the squatter settlements express the general problem of homelessness and housing crisis, a sound conceptualization should also include the population of homeless people who have not yet built their residential sites in the city. An empirically valid definition of squatter settlement should also embrace the recently growing population of absolutely homeless urban "dwellers."

Unfortunately, despite the power of Abrams' conceptualization of squatter settlements, this important form of housing crisis is not included. A broad and comprehensive conceptualization of squatter settlements should not only deal with property relations (e.g., the degree of violation of institutionalized private property relations) but also must include those dimensions that directly measure the degree of access to infrastructural services and economic opportunities. At least these three factors then would seem to differ from settlement to settlement: (1) the degree of institutionalization and connection with the "formal" city; (2) the economic roles of the squatter dwellers; (3) the nature of property relation and class conflict implied by the settlement.

In summary, the *squatter settlements, here, broadly refer to diverse forms of marginal settlements that have some basic problems of infrastructural urban facilities; the majority of residents suffer from land tenure insecurity; and most of the residents belong to the bottom of the socio-economic hierarchy.* For operational purpose in this study, the basic infrastructural urban facilities refer to piped water, electricity, and the quality of materials used in the construction of houses. Tenure security refers to the legal position of residents from the view point of the state. Socio-economic status refers to the residents' level of monthly income, literacy, and origin (migrants or non-migrants).

Usually, the correlations among the major dimensions of squatter settlements are strong. Nonetheless, each one is autonomous and therefore produces an empirically unique settlement. Consequently, each empirical squatter settlement can be located within a three dimensional structure representing the general phenomenon of housing crisis. The result is presented in table 7.1.

As the table shows, the beginning of the spectrum embraces those squatter settlements that are fully marginalized at all dimensions; the end of the spectrum represents typical well-established urban dwellers. The existing empirical settlements fall, in terms of the degree of marginalization, between the beginning and the end of the three dimensional

Table 7.1

A Multidimensional Model For the Identification of Various Forms of Squatter Settlements

Property Relations	The Degree of Land Insecurity	High	Low
Access to Urban Services & Connection to Urban System	Access to Piped Water	Low	High
	Access to Electricity	Low	High
	Durable Construction Materials Used in Residential Units	Low	High
Socio-Economic Status (Class Position and Economic Role)	Ratio of Rural Migrants in Community	High	Low
	Rate of Literacy Among Residents	Low	High
	Average Income Level in Community	Low	High
Overall Typification		Homeless Rural Migrants	Regular Urban Residents

spectrum.

There are a number of advantages to the use of this spectrum. First, it is possible to locate and identify various marginal settlements with a uniform set of criteria. Second, future research can become more cumulative and comparative so that meaningful cross-cultural studies would be practical. Third, "the scope conditions" of employed concepts would be wide and comprehensive so that all empirical settlements in relation to housing crisis will be included . Fourth, the level of marginalization of each community can be calculated vis-a-vis other settlements so that meaningful policy recommendations (e.g., community upgrading) can be orchestrated along each dimension. The use of a summative scale of normalized (Z-scored) may be used to estimate the level of marginalization for every component of the typology. What follows is the application of this method to the major squatter settlements in Iran, in term of its internal variation and the level of marginalization. The typology will be used to understand the real differences among the Iranian squatters.

The Dimensions of Squatter Settlements in Iran

Based on the typology presented in table 7.1, 9 previously studied squatter settlements were selected and their major features in terms of property relations, infrastructural facilities, and socio-economic status were identified.[1] The result is presented in table 7.2. Table shows great diversity in the internal composition of settlements at the level of infrastructural, socio-economic, and property relations. The settlements can be roughly classified by Turner's approach emphasizing the degree of institutionalization/marginalization.

"Zoor Abad" squatters portray characteristics similar to what Turner describes as consolidators. The settlement shelters more than 50,000 homeless people and scores high on infrastructural as well as on socio-economic dimensions. However, in terms of property relations, the settlement is more like a "bridgeheader" than a "consolidator" since the residents have no legal right to the land on which they live.

This community grew quite rapidly after the revolution in 1979 and the majority of residents forcefully preempted land owned by the

---

[1]I chose those studies that had the most information on the three dimensions of settlements causing the most critical variations in the internal structure of squatters. If the reader needs a list (bibliography) of all Persian speaking publications on squatter settlements of Iran, she/he may use this source: Abol Hassan Danesh:" Mooghadame'e bar Teory Moohajert-hayee Bee Raveeyeh va Hasheeh Nesheenee dar Keshvarhayee Je-han-e Sevvom: Yek motaleh Moredey dar Iran. Plan and Budget Organization, Tehran, Iran (in

state. In fact, the term "Zoor" in the Persian language means "force and power" and "Abad" usually refers to a recently formed small village or urban community. The residents of Zoor Abad are exceptionally militant and unlike other squatters know how to use and manipulate the available institutional resources at the right time and at the right place. The residents, for example, decided to replace the antagonizing name of "Zoor Abad" with a diplomatic one, "Islam Abad", after the Islamic revolution. The residential units are build on two medium-size hills which are located at the north edge of Karaj city, 15 miles west of Tehran. The land has a relatively high value, and a beautiful view. Whereever you are in Karaj city, you are able to see the crowded face of the Zoor Abad community right upon the hills. Some of the residents are recruited from the lower rank of the Islamic revolutionary guard (e.g., Pasdaran, Islamic Committee), which fortifies the community against potential State's intruders who, in the name of "green space," would like to bulldozer the community at any minute.

In contrast, "Kappar Nesheenun," the major squatter settlement in Bandar Abas, a southern city near the Persian Gulf, despite its long history, is extremely poor. The community has minimal access to the necessary infrastructural facilities and socio-economic resources. While large numbers of residents are urban born dwellers (45 percent of residents had rural origin), the settlement in relation to the dimensions of infrastructural facilities and socio-economic resources is quite similar to Turner's description of "bridgeheaders." For example, only 2 percent of residents have electricity, 2 percent have piped water, and only about 5 percent of all construction materials are durable (the remaining 95 percent are made of straw and various discarded materials such as dead battery and used plastic). The literacy level is low and only 25 percent of residents can read or write; in terms of income level the community also scores the lowest among our selected sample.

The "Goed Nesheenun" is another major squatter settlement in Iran, and on the average is less integrated than the "Zoor Abad" but more integrated than the "Kappar Nesheenun." As its local name implies, the settlement is located in the heart of a gigantic "hole", formed by brick-making industries in southern Tehran. It is almost an underground residential community and is extremely vulnerable to rain and snow. Its population is very diverse in terms of origin, occupational structure, and ethnic composition. The settlement is composed of 15 interconnected sub-communities which together shelters 1,040 households with 46,210 residents. It is very crowded, and the residents use every inch of the available space. In fact, those households that have

Persian only), 1984.

Table 7.2

Multidimensional Profiles of 9 Selected Squatter Settlements in Iran

Location of squatter settlement and its local name	Access to Urban Infrastructural Facilities			Socio-Economic Status			Property Relations	
	Percentage households have access to pipe water	Percentage households have access to electricity	Percentage durable materials used in building	Percentage literacy among residents	Percentage rural residents in community	Monthly ave. income per household (rial)	Legal status of community in city	Date research completed
Zoor Abad-e Karaj (Islam-Abad)	15.6%	96.3%	91.5%	N/A	N/A	20370	LOW	1981
Go-od Ne-sherun Tehran	59.1%	N/A	78.2%	53.0%	36.3%	N/A	LOW	1980
Ka-par-ne-sherun Bandar-Abbas	2.0%	2.0%	5.0%	26.0%	48.6%	2180	LOW	1972
Ka-par-ne-sherun Iran-Shahr	less than 1.0%	N/A	less than 1.0%	N/A	46.0%	2490	LOW	1975
Ta-peh-ne-sherun Naqadeh	34.5%	16.0%	32.8%	33.0%	52.0%	5700	HIGH	1975
Ka-par-ne-sherun Bandar Boo-shehr	N/A	N/A	7.0%	17.0%	42.6%	2700	LOW	1976
Ila-sheh-ne-sherun Kerman-shah	17.0%	3.0%	7.0%	37.0%	52.0%	2590	LOW	1977
Ila-sheh-ne-sherun Ah-vas	24.0%	61.0%	13.0%	27.0%	41.0%	4000	LOW	1977
Ila-sheh-ne-sherun Tehran	5.0%	6.0%	11.0%	N/A	40.0%	N/A	LOW	1973

Source: Abol Hassan Danesh, An Introduction to a Theory of Irregular Rural-Urban Migration in Developing Countries: A Case Study in Iran. Plan and Budget Organization, Tehran (In Persian only), 1984.

only one room or less comprise more than 64 percent of all households in the community. The mean is 15.6 square meters per room.

The characteristics of the remaining squatter settlements in various parts of Iran are presented in table 7.2, which shows that values on one dimension do not always correspond to values on other dimensions. The three-dimension model produces different rankings and further proves that Turner's view is not sophisticated enough to reflect all forms of squatter settlements in the context of the housing crisis in Iran. The proposed model, however, is capable of generating endless logical combinations of settlements, many of which may not have empirical referents. What follows is an effort to modify the model to fit the major forms of squatter settlements across the developing countries.

Variation in Iranian Squatter Settlements

Unidimensional typologies, like Turner's, do not do justice to the true variablity in squatter settlements. Popular and journalistic imageries of the social and economic structures of squatter settlements and their residents are even less adequate. There are a number of publically held mystified images about the conditions and characteristics of the squatter dwellers. Usually in the press, the residents are portrayed as unemployed illiterates who have migrated recently from the rural areas. It is often said that the dwellers build their shacks around the growing cities with the left-overs of industries, and other discarded materials. It is also portrayed that the residents have illegally occupied the land on which they live (Mangin, 1968). It has been argued that the residents have non-considerable linkages with the formal economy and they are viewed by the middle class as superfluous and parasitical. Some writers go even so far as to describe the formation of squatter settlements as the inevitable cost of industrialization in the Third World (Adams, 1974).

Each of the elements of the popular stereotype has some validity but much of that is unrelated to squatter settlements in Iran. The author in his examination of major squatter settlements in Iran found that there are *distinctly* different types of settlements.

First, the origin of residents varies drastically from one settlement to another. In some cases, the majority of residents are rural migrants and in other cases the majority are urban dwellers who have escaped from inner city more costly conventional housing. For example, approximately 75 percent of "Goed Nesheenun" was made of those dwellers who were not rural migrants (A. Khorasaneezadeh, 1980). Similarly, about 60 percent of the residents of "Hasheh Nesheenun" in Tehran city did not have rural backgrounds. In my case study of "Tarasht"

132

community in 1983, the heads of households who had rural backgrounds comprised 41 percent of the residents. This rate would be significantly less if one adds the children to the community population.

Second, all who reside in squatter settlements do not necessarily belong to marginal or low income jobs. Similarly, those who live in regular housing do not always hold non-marginal and high income jobs. In other words, the nature of residential place (squatter versus regular housing) does not fully predict and explain one's level of economic integration and income. For example in the case of "Zoor Abad", the available data suggest that more than 20 percent of the active population were engaged in the manufacturing sector. Similarly, the residents of "Goed Nesheenun" were not all marginals; approximately 57 percent were in productive enterprises in 1980. My field work of "Tarasht" squatters showed just the opposite. More than 90 percent of all household heads were in casual and unproductive jobs in the informal and underground economy.

These relatively surprising findings are embedded in the peculiarities of the Iranian socio-economic system. There is a relatively weak correspondence between the level of one's job productivity and his income level. In other words, the level of integration, here defined as one's level of marginal productivity in the formal or informal economy, is not a good predictor of one's economic opportunities. In many instances, the author observed urban dwellers, working in quite unproductive and parasitical jobs in the informal economy, with incomes surpassing the salary of professional employees in the formal economy (some of whom had Ph.D.'s in their professions).[2]

Thus, the squatter settlement is a variable phenomenon and one way to de-mystify the empirically unfounded stereotypes is to treat its various components as autonomous entities for every concrete setting. Four dimensions have been identified which are very helpful to locate and identify Iranian squatter settlements: a. the level of integration in the urban economy (economic status); b. the housing conditions of the residents in relation to access to urban infrastructural facilities; c. the origin of dwellers (rural versus urban- social status); and d. property relations which express the legal position of the settlement from the standpoint of the state. Dimensions "a" and "c" together represent one's socio-economic status and are separated from each other in order to evaluate the role of rural-urban migration in squatter settlements. The mixture of these four dimensions identifies 12 major forms of empirical urban settlements, some of which have not been identified in the

---

[2]For more information on the relation between employment in the informal service sector and income in Iran see: Abol Hassan Danesh: Elal va Avamele Goustaresh-e Mashaghele Kazeb dar Shahr-hayee Boozorg. Plan and Budget Organization, Tehran Iran (in Persian) 1984.

literature.[3] This diversity of squatter settlements in Iran is expressed in Table 7.3.

Type 1 through type 4 in the table represent regular housing in the cities of Iran with major variations on residents' place of origin and socio-economic status. For example type 1 shows an unusual case where the recently rural migrants, despite lack of integration in the urban economy, live in regular housing with access to good infrastructural facilities. While this case might be very rare in many developing countries, it was very common in Tehran city during the revolutionary period. After the outbreak of revolution in 1979, many well-to-do upper

Table 7.3

Typology of Urban Residents Based on Their Place in Urban Economy, Regional Origin, Type of Housing and Relations in Iran

	Origin of Residents			
	RURAL		URBAN	
	LEVEL OF INTEGRATION IN URBAN ECONOMY		LEVEL OF INTEGRATION IN URBAN ECONOMY	
	LOW	HIGH	LOW	HIGH
LEVEL OF ACCESS TO URBAN INFRASTRUCTURAL FACILITIES	(1) Rural migrants not integrated in urban economy & settled in regular housing	(2) Rural migrants settled in regular housing, integrated in economy, & live in regular housing	(3) Non-migrant urban dwellers not integrated in economy & live in regular housing	(4) Typical non-migrant urban middle class who have high paying jobs and live in regular housing
	Rural migrants not integrated in urban economy & live in squatter settlements	Rural migrants integrated in urban economy & live in squatter settlements	Non-migrant urban residents not integrated in urban economy but resided in squatter settlements	Non-migrant urban dwellers integrated in urban economy but resided in squatter settlements
	5 legal	6 Illegal	7 legal	8 Illegal	9 legal	10 Illegal	11 legal	12 Illegal
	PROPERTY RELATIONS			

* Of course, it is not assumed that each type is internally homogeneous. In fact, some minor variations exist within each type too. However, further logical extension of this schematic typology leads to the loss of its theoretical rigor. In my opinion, excessive extension of discretionary typology culminates in an absurd and useless hairsplitting classification.

and middle class Iranians fled the country leaving some of the wealth and property behind. It was a rare opportunity for the poor and unemployed rural migrants to capitalize on this situation. During the revolutionary period, any homeless person who could find a vacant house or building could expropriate it individually or collectively. In some cases, they struggled against the will of other tenants to bring their sheeps or donkeys to their seized fancy apartment on the 10th floor! What an inconsistency in one's life style!

Type 3 reflects the similar situation for the urban dwellers who forcefully took over the left-behind-apartment and housing properties.[4] Types 2 and 4 should be understood without any difficulty since they refer to those established city dwellers with good housing and well-paying secure jobs.

The remaining typology embraces eight different types of squatters. While all of them suffer from the lack of basic infrastructural urban amenities and social services (to different degrees), they vary on the origin, property relations, and integration in the urban economy.

Type 5 and type 9 represent those legal squatter settlements whose residents are not absorbed by the urban economy and who do not hold productive jobs in the society. Type 9 differs from type 5 only on the dimension of origin. The former usually embraces the poor and unemployed urban dwellers in inner city "slums" who have to pay rent to their legal landlords. The latter refers to those inner-city slum communities whose residents are predominantly rural. Many of these non-integrated poor residents of inner-city slums, who had extensive contact with urban institutions, took advantage of the legal momentum of housing ownership created by the revolution. Some of them made themselves home-owner by invading and possessing the vacant buildings left behind by the allies of the old regime. These people shifted their structural location from type 5 and type 9 to type 1 and type 3 during the revolutionary period. Other moved to type 6 and type 10 in order to build their shacks on empty lands. The volume of this form of squatter settlement was phenomenal. The "Zoor Abad" settlement, with 40,000 inhabitants, was only one among many other communities that mushroomed in pre-and post-revolutionary periods.

Type 6 has been an especially dominant form in Latin America, and is becoming predominant in Iran. This type and type 10 score very low on every dimensions of squatter settlements and are often picked up by journalists and "pop" sociology as a model to describe and talk about

---

[4]It is expected that the institutionalization of revolution in Iran will increasingly limit the growth of this form of squatting. In fact, some drastic measures have already been taken against property-invaders in the realm of housing. However, it is expected that any society, especially the today's developing countries with major socio-economic crises, would greatly experience this form of urban struggle in the field of housing.

shantytowns and squatter settlements in the developing countries.

Type 7 and type 11 show still other forms of squatter settlements. Such communities embrace individuals who are either rural migrants or urban born city dwellers who have been geared to the urban economy but are unable to find regular housing in the city. As far as the problems of housing scarcity in general and squatter settlement in particular are concerned, the very existence of these forms of squatter, especially type 11, provides an important insight about the nature of social inequality in society. That is, when a sizable portion of urban inhabitants has been located in this housing category, one can strongly argue that the housing scarcity has reached a level that not only hits the low income groups but also has effectively pushed the regular and relatively well-established lower middle income groups toward the squatter settlements. Under these conditions, formation of squatter settlements is no longer abnormal but a vital solution to rapid urbanization and housing crisis.

In the case of Iran it was found that many urban dwellers who were born in the cities and had productive functions in the urban economy had to choose, reluctantly, to live in squatter settlements. In fact, it can be argued that the excessive influx of rural migrants in the metropolitan cities, coupled with inadequate production of infrastructural facilities, has also pushed the regular urban dwellers toward the squatter settlements.[5]

Finally, type 8 and type 12 represent those squatter settlements that are not legally accepted by the government, but include inhabitants that are mostly integrated into the urban economy. It is expected that when the government officials recognize the legality of such settlements, residents will rapidly upgrade their community. This form of settlement is attractive to those individuals who are unable to pay a rent; they are willing to challenge and resist the state's intimidation. For them, the squatter settlement is not only a place to live and raise children but also a place to prove one's sense of manhood and independence.

---

[5]These two types of residential communities are quite common among professional and relatively well-educated residents of the south-west provinces of Iran. The reason is that the continuing war between Iran and Iraq had badly damaged both the cities and their peoples. It has been reported that more than 1.5 million people have become homeless as the result of this bloody war in 1984. Close to 70 percent of all war victims are in the southwestern provinces. In addition to the effect of war on the housing conditions, it has been reported by the Iranian officials that more than 2 million Afghani refugees have legally or illegally joined the main cities of Iran, causing an untolerable pressure on the housing market in the country.

Conclusion

Any serious research on squatter settlements in the Third World should pay attention to some major pitfalls mentioned here. Squatter settlements, contrary to its simplified name, is a very complex and heterogeneous phenomenon resulting from the growing housing crisis. It was shown that the residents of squatter settlements have very diversified backgrounds. The synthesis of various studies conducted in Iran show that property relations (e.g., legal aspects of the settlement), economic functions of residents (e.g., income, literacy rate, participation in formal and informal economy, productive or non-productive function in urban society), and residents' origin (e.g., rural and urban), are not constant among all settlements and among the residents of the settlements. These differences are important in understanding how the social problem, needs, and policy preferences should differ from town to town to town.[6]

Field-based descriptions of squatter settlements raise the question as to whether the dichotomy of squatter settlements fits the facts. The author's study in post revolutionary Iran finds no "simple" dichotomy between squatter settlements recently established by the rural migrants, and well established urban settlements, but a multidimensional continuum on which 12 major forms are placed in order. Especially among the illegal squatter settlements whose land tenure is shaky, the struggle for shelter and survival is intense and often assume collective form to the point where it can make a significant difference for political outcomes and revolutionary change. Given the socio-political significance of squatter settlements, it is fruitful to examine the general problem of housing crisis from which squatter settlements in their diverse forms emerge. The examination will be limited to the problem of housing in Tehran city, as described by census data.

---

[6]Insensitivity to this important fact has led to a growing conflict in the conclusions made about squatter dwellers in the literature. For example, Janice Perlman in her influencial book, *The Myth of Marginality,* uncritically concludes that all squatter dwellers are or will be integrated in the urban economy and therefore the term "marginality" does not correctly depict the situations of the squatter dwellers. In contrast, Lominitz in her study of shantytowns in Mexico makes the unwarranted generalization that the dwellers are predominantly marginal and poor. Again, these contradictory generalizations and conclusions stem from the very fact that there are different types of squatter settlements and each has its own specification. In other words, there are both integrated and non-integrated squatter settlements in the urban system; there are poor as well as relatively well-off residents in various squatter settlements; and thus because of this heterogeneity, generalization about squatter settlements is quite unrealistic.

CHAPTER VIII

CONSEQUENCES OF IRREGULAR
RURAL-URBAN MIGRATION:
HOUSING CRISIS

In the previous chapter, the problem of squatter settlements as one of the most important effects of irregular migration was examined. In this chapter the focus will be on the more general problem of urban conditions within which squatter settlements are structurally produced and located. This general problem of urban conditions is the "housing crisis." In what follows the form and extent of the housing crisis, in the context of irregular migration, will be studied in Iran in general and in Tehran city in particular.

Based on conservative estimates, the housing shortage has been a very acute problem in most urban regions. It is believed that in 1978 Iranian cities were approximately 925,000 housing units short of the demand made by urban dwellers (Mashhoodee, 1980). Assuming that each house sheltered between five and ten people, the number of home-less urban dwellers would be between 4.6 to 9.2 million people. During 1979-1979 there were 17 million urban residents throughout the country; it can be concluded that 27 to 54 percent of all urban residents have remained homeless in the urban centers.

To eradicate the problem of housing shortage in urban centers completely by the year 1988, it is necessary to build as many as 340,000 residential units for the entire urban homeless Iranian population. It is impossible to reach such a goal, since the maximum number of houses ever made in Iran (in 1975, during oil boom)was not more than 182,000 units. Spending more than 10 percent of the G.N.P. on the housing industry stagnates in the long run the more vital industrial and commercial units.[1]

---

[1]Of course this estimation of housing shortage is too optimistic and does not take into account those variables that have greatly enhanced the housing shortage in the post-revolutionary period. Two important factors have been the source of bias in projecting the housing shortages for the year 1988: 1) Iran-Iraq war; 2) immigration of national Afghani to Iran during 1980-1985. These two factors have significantly accelerated the chronic problems of housing in the subsequent years. Also, the situation of war, departure of

The shortage of housing does not affect all urban residents equally. The poor urban dwellers and rural migrants are the major victims of the housing crisis. Studies on the housing shortage in urban centers are very scarce. The only available comprehensive investigation, in 1966, lends support to the argument. It was found that the low income group in Tehran city was faced with a massive housing shortage. In Tehran city alone, the demand made by the low income group exceeded the supply by 78,000 housing units while the upper income group had 14,000 surplus houses. At that time, more than 44 percent of all Tehran's residents were in the low income category, whereas the upper income group comprised only 1 percent of Tehran's entire population. Table 8.1 demonstrates the distribution of population and dwelling units among four major income groups in Tehran city in 1966. Kazemi's studies also represent similar relations.

The general housing shortage on the one hand, and the unequal distribution of the available housing units on the other hand, seem to have accelerated in the subsequent years. Certainly, the massive destruction of houses in the Iran-Iraq war and the immigration of large numbers of Afghani rebels to Iran have aggravated the effects of rural influx on the housing shortage. Even ignoring cataclysmic impacts of these events, the increasing land speculation, as an easy route to the accumulation of wealth, has unquestionably restrained the egalitarian distribution of the existing dwelling units among the lower income groups. Kazemi observes this important aspect of housing crisis and adds:

> This deficiency greatly increased in the 1970's as land speculation
> raised the price of housing unrealistically. In addition, problems in
> distribution of electricity and water, inadequate public transportation
> facilities, and other such amenities have made life for the residents of
> Tehran excessively difficult (Kazemi, 1981).

In addition to land speculation and unequal distribution of housing units, the available data on the construction of housing units in Tehran and other urban regions also show that despite the growing influx of

---

foreign engineers and construction workers, economic blockage, and insufficient raw materials in construction industry badly hurt this vital economic sector in Iran sine the beginning of the revolution.

The impact of recent war on Iranian society is diverse indeed but as far as the problem of housing is concerned the war has destroyed as many as 350,000 residential units most of which were in Khouzistan province. In addition to this direct effect of war on the housing shortage and homelessness, the war has also reduced the production capacity of those manufacturing units which supply consumption and intermediary goods for the construction industry (e.g., brickmaking industry, Iran's bar and concrete industry). On the other hand, most of the Iranian borders have been left quite open to Moslem Afghani nationals who have fled their homeland after the establishment of a pro-Soviet State in Afghanistan. Although there is no official record of Afghani refugees in Iran (most of them are undocumented workers); many Iranian officials (e.g., Mayor of Tehran city) believe that the to-

Table 8.1

Estimated Distribution of Families and Ownership of Dwelling Units in Four Income Groups of Tehran in 1966

Income Group	Number of Families	Number of Dwelling Units
Low Income	278,000 (44%)	200,000 (35%)
Low Middle Income	278,000 (44%)	280,000 (49%)
Upper Middle Income	69,000 (11%)	70,000 (12.3%)
High Income	6,000 (1%)	20,000 (4%)
TOTAL	631,000 (100%)	570,000 (100%)

Source: Iran, Economic Survey of Greater Tehran, Tehran, Iran, 1966.

rural migrants and despite the rapid natural population growth in Tehran city, the share of the private construction industry in building new houses continuously declined in Tehran city vis-a-vis other urban regions. That is, Tehran city, despite its rapid population growth, due primarily to migration, was unable to allocate a similar proportion of

tal number is between 1.8 and 3 million refugee people.

investment for the housing industry.

The share of the private sector in the construction industry, which produces up to 90 percent of residential housing units in the country, systematically declined in Tehran city. In 1975, based on the number of construction permissions issued by the City Hall in all Iranian urban centers, approximately 43 percent of all "housing spaces" (in terms of square meter) was the share of Tehran city. The share of other large cities was only 27.2 percent, and the remaining small size urban centers had access only to 29 percent of housing units; in this year, Tehran city officially allowed the construction agencies to build about 17, 379 square meters in all urban centers.

This composition of housing distribution, however, changes at the expense of Tehran city both relatively and absolutely. In 1979, the share of Tehran declined to 20.8 percent of the housing space permitted by the City Hall. Given the fact that the private sector produces houses largely for the high and middle income groups, one can easily understand the extraordinary magnitude of the housing shortage for the low income groups in major urban centers in general, and in Tehran in particular during 1955-1979. Table 8.2 shows the distribution of housing units in Tehran city, in all large urban centers, and in all small cities during 1975-1979.

Table 8.2 also demonstrates the distribution of dwelling units that were completed by private owners and private corporations. The data show a similar pattern and indicate that despite the growing population in Tehran city and despite the extraordinary volume of rural migrants, each year the gap between the demand and supply in the housing market increased, particularly among the low income groups. Except in 1979, which is associated with the breakdown of the state and increasing organized political demand-making on the housing market, the data clearly and systematically demonstrate that Tehran city's share of dwelling units declined during 1975-1979. The share of Tehran was 35.6 percent in 1975 and 24.9 percent in 1978. The total housing space that was constructed in 1975, 1976, 1977, 1978, and 1979 was 14951, 16114, 18851, 20984, and 24686 square meters for the corresponding years (for more detailed information see table 8.2).

The nature of the housing industry in and of itself has also contributed to the general situation of housing scarcity in the major urban centers in Iran and has put an additional burden on the urban poor. It is therefore necessary to examine the features of the construction sector itself and how it has accelerated the existing conditions of the housing shortage.

Table 8.2
Square Meters of Housing Constructed in Urban Areas in Iran During 1975-1979

		1975	1976	1977	1978	1979
Based on Documentary Permission Issued by the City's Municipal	Tehran	7,615 (43.8%)	8,534.6 (35.2%)	5,093.2 (30.7%)	5,057.3 (30.6%)	4,598.4 (20.8%)
	Other Large Cities in Iran	4,729.9 (27.2%)	7,468.5 (30.8%)	5,276.3 (31.9%)	5,119.3 (31.0%)	8,017.3 (35.2%)
	All Small Cities in Iran	5,035.7 (29%)	8,264.9 (34.0%)	6,231.2 (37.4%)	6,349.0 (38.4%)	10,177.1 (45.0%)
	All Cities	17,379.6 (100%)	24,268 (100%)	16,600.8 (100%)	16,525.6 (100%)	22,792.8 (100%)
Houses completed by private owners & private corporations	Tehran	5,327 (35.6%)	5,340 (33.1%)	5,555 (29.5%)	5,212 (24.9%)	7,844 (31.8%)
	Other Large Cities in Iran	5,175 (34.6%)	4,634 (28.7%)	5,861 (31.1%)	6,562 (31.3%)	7,909 (32.0%)
	All Small Cities in Iran	4,449 (29.8%)	6,140 (38.2%)	7,436 (39.4%)	9,210 (43.8%)	8,933 (36.2%)
	All Cities	14,951 (100%)	16,114 (100%)	18,851 (100%)	20,984 (100%)	24,686 (100%)

Source: Calculations based on Ve-za-ra-te Mas-kan Va Shahr-sa-zee, 1980, 1981.

Housing Shortage and Housing Industry

The housing industry is unique and in many significant ways differs from other industries. The uniqueness of the housing industry should be found in its mode of production and distribution in the urban centers.

First, housing scarcity, unlike other commodities, not only touches the poor but also is the concern of many lower and middle income groups as well. Given the fact that "shelter" is absolutely a necessary condition for the reproduction of labor, disruption in production and distribution of such a commodity has severe consequences for the existing social and political systems.

Second, houses are built on the land, and cannot be moved around easily. The relative immobility of housing units in space causes a great level of stagnation in the very process of production/distribution of products in the market. It is not often observed that the inconsistency between the mobility of labor on the one hand and the geographical immobility of houses and buildings on the other hand is one of the primary reasons for land speculation which has, in return, aggravated the shortage for a great number of people.

Third, the housing industry, in contrast to the production of other commodities, such as the car, is not easily subject to standardization and routinization of production. To build a house it is necessary to provide and organize a large number of items of production, many of which cannot be fabricated. They must be arranged and produced spontaneously at the site of building. Except for the housing industry in the US, this industry is conspicuously primitive and yet quite delicate in many developed and underdeveloped countries.

Fourth, labor in the construction industry is relatively spontaneous, and it is quite impractical to apply control and supervision, labeled as scientific management, to the labor. Castells observes this important relation in the construction sector and adds:

> Such a situation, in interaction with the very characteristics of the labor process, which make less easy than elsewhere the mechanization and standardization of operations, gives rise to what is very often an archaic form of industrialization. Activity splits up between a multitude of small companies, a low rate of technological innovation, a low level of training among the workers and, above all, a low number of workers per company
> (in relation to other branches of industry), which limits proportionally the sources of surplus value, diminishes profit, increases cost and discourages investment. All these characteristics taken together lead to low productivity which, in return, perpetuates the shortage (M. Castells, 1979:153-4).

Particularly in Iran, these peculiarities of the construction industry, in conjunction with unrestained land speculation, low private investment, and migration, have discouraged any organized efforts on the part of the state and private investors to relieve the housing crisis. The shortage after the oil boom became so severe that the increasing price in the housing market led many previous squatter dwellers, sheltered by the state-sponsored cheap housing project, to sell their real estate to middle class residents. It is reported that many ex-squatters who were housed in the "Koye Nohome Aban" sold their regular houses and rejoined the squatter dwellers.[2]

The effectiveness of the response to the housing shortage is not well-known. Unfortunately, after the 1966 comprehensive survey on the housing situation in Tehran city, no other similar research has been carried out to identify the form and the magnitude of the housing shortage, nor the surplus among various income groups. However, an attempt can be made to estimate the volume of housing shortage by using and reconstructing the available census data in 1966 and 1976. The remainder of this chapter will be devoted to this task by using various indicators of housing shortages in various regions of Tehran city. These indicators represent the level of crowding (lack of adequate space), sub-standard housing, use of non-durable construction materials in the building, and houses that are considered squatter settlements by the census. These indicators systematically underestimates the level of housing shortages; because many of urban residents who live and sleep in "hidden squatters" (basically the street homeless people) have no reflection in official statistics.

Shortage in Space and Overcrowding

One of the main characteristics of homelessness in general and squatter settlements in particular is the inadequacy of space in which people live. That is to say, overcrowding can be considered an indicator of housing shortages. According to the United Nations' criterion, overcrowding occurs when three or more individuals live in one room. Using this criterion of overcrowding in Tehran city, the author's calculations show that more than 200,000 people lived in that environment. This figure represents more than 4 percent of the population in Tehran

---

[2]This occurs especially when the value of a house in the market is not proportional to the overall revenue of the household. Many squatter dwellers are unemployed and poor, and it is expected that when they receive housing from the government they tend to sell it back in the highly demanded housing market. With that money they can buy another shack in another part of squatter settlement plus they can pay back their debts and maybe put the remaining cash into a new business.

in 1976. At that time, Tehran embraced more than 4.5 million people. In table 8.3 the pattern of housing shortages in 12 independent districts in Tehran is shown. The indicator of overcrowding shows that district 7 embraced the greatest number of overcrowded communities in the city and districts 4 and 6 were the second and third crowdedest regions in the capital. These three districts have been traditionally the seats for poor and uprooted people in Tehran city.

Table 8.3

Selected Indicators for the Estimation of Housing Shortages and Squatter Settlements in Tehran City, Iran, 1976

Region	Population	% born in Tehran City	Distribution of pop. in each region	(1) Crowded housing (1 rm. for more than 3 people)	(2) % of households live in non-standard houses	(3) Number of households live in squatters	(4) Number of houses made of non-durable materials	Number of economically active pop. who are unemployed or non-classifiable
Tehran 1977	4,530,223	55.1	100%	200,223	1%	4,181	5,924	193,474
Region 1	508,704	51.3	11%	10,615	0.9%	318	221	23,363
Region 2	136,428	51.4	3%	1,905	2.7%	240	425	25,487
Region 3	260,918	54.3	6%	17,643	0.6%	102	214	26,028
Region 4	622,724	53.3	14%	37,279	1.8%	805	697	17,913
Region 5	317,842	56.5	7%	18,241	1.7%	310	1,241	8,364
Region 6	695,485	60.8	15%	33,958	1.0%	776	1,198	16,406
Region 7	496,597	51.6	11%	39,122	0.6%	294	331	10,597
Region 8	478,269	56.5	12%	14,186	1.5%	728	639	28,823
Region 9	202,795	52.4	4%	1,610	1.2%	169	142	10,622
Region 10	333,200	55.8	7%	7,911	0.9%	197	448	41,358
Region 11	42,057	55.2	1%	1,784	3.7%	67	118	942
Region 12	215,789	58.2	5%	15,968	0.7%	175	561	6,848
Tehran 1967	2,719,730	51.1	N/A	155,668	N/A	N/A	15,030	N/A

Source: Calculated based on information and data provided by Census, 1966, 1976, Iran.

145

Low Standard Housing

The 1976 census also provides information for those individuals who have lived in shelters characterized as "non-standard." Unfortunately, the census did not specify what criterion is used to delineate non-standard housing from standard. Thus, it is important to interpret these data with some caution and care.

Overall, the census showed that more than one percent of the population lived in such housing and that some districts in Tehran city had a disproportionate share of this form of inadequate housing. Districts 11, 2, and 4 embraced the greatest number of low standard housing; districts 3 and 12 embraced the least number of low standard housing.

Houses Classified as "Squatters"

It is possible to obtain information from the census about the number of urban dwellers who lived in residential units considered by the Bureau of Statistical Center in Iran as "unconventional." Without offering any definition as to what constitutes unconventionality of housing units, the census estimated that more than 4,181 households resided in the following dwellings; the author provides a brief description of them:

A. "**Chador**" is similar to a camping tent and is often built on a relatively solid foundation.

B. "**Zagheh**" is a temporary residential unit made of mud, clay, and other similar earthenware.

C. "**Alonack**" is similar to Zagheh and usually refers to a small, unstable, and dark room. Alonack, due to its primitive nature, is devoid of windows, and discarded materials such as dead automobile batteries, cardboard, and empty food or oil containers are used in its construction. One room in and of itself constitutes one Alonack and it is considered among the squatter dwellers as an autonomous residential unit. If the necessary construction materials are readily available, the construction of an Alonack can be completed by two adult individuals in a matter of two or three days.

D. "**Kappar**" is an extremely primitive dwelling unit and is usually found in the impoverished southern part of Iran. The walls and roof are mostly made of leaves and branches of tropical trees or straw. Some Kappar, especially in the cities of Bandar Abas and Bandar Bosheher, are built beneath the ground in order to resist the extreme temperature in summer. However, the underground Kappar is

146

exceptionally vulnerable to seasonal rain and flood.

Table 8.3 assembles the necessary information about the distribution of these squatter type houses for 12 districts in Tehran in 1976, and demonstrates that district 4 contained the largest number of unconventional city dwellers. Tehran city as a whole embraced about 808 households living in Kappar, Zagheh, Alonack, and Chador.

Houses Made of Non-durable Construction Materials

The census used the type of construction materials used in the actual production of houses as an indicator of sub-standard dwelling units. It is important, however, to note that the Iranian census did not indicate the criterion which was used for the operational definition of nondurable construction materials. Assuming that each average residential unit could have sheltered six people, overall more than 40,000 people lived in such houses that were made of discarded materials, clay, cardboard, and other similar earthenware items. The distribution of this type of residential unit in each of the 12 districts of Tehran city in 1976 is shown in table 8.3.

Assuming that all four indicators of squatter housing are mutually exclusive and exhaustive, by adding columns 1, 2, 3, and 4 one may conclude that more than 750,000 people lived and struggled in squatter-type-settlements (see the definition in chapter 7) in Tehran city. The assumption of exclusiveness and exhaustiveness of indicators of squatter settlements is not perfectly met in all instances by the census bureau in Iran and, thus, the author's estimation could vary as much as 100,000 units from the actual population of the squatter settlements in Tehran city.

The last column in table 8.3 represents the size of the economically marginal population in 12 districts of Tehran city. If the economically marginal population is defined as those economically active who are either unemployed or whose jobs are considered as unclassifiable, table 8.3 demonstrates that more than 190,000 people belong to this economic category. The distribution of the economically marginal population in 12 districts of Tehran city shows a considerable level of correspondence between the squatter population and economic marginality in each district. It is often said that the southern districts are predominantly poor, and the analysis of the census data shows that the majority of people in these areas have been not only homeless but also unemployed and detached from the urban economy.

Diagram 8.1

The Role of the State, Rural Exodus, and Power in the
Formation of Squatter Settlements in Iran

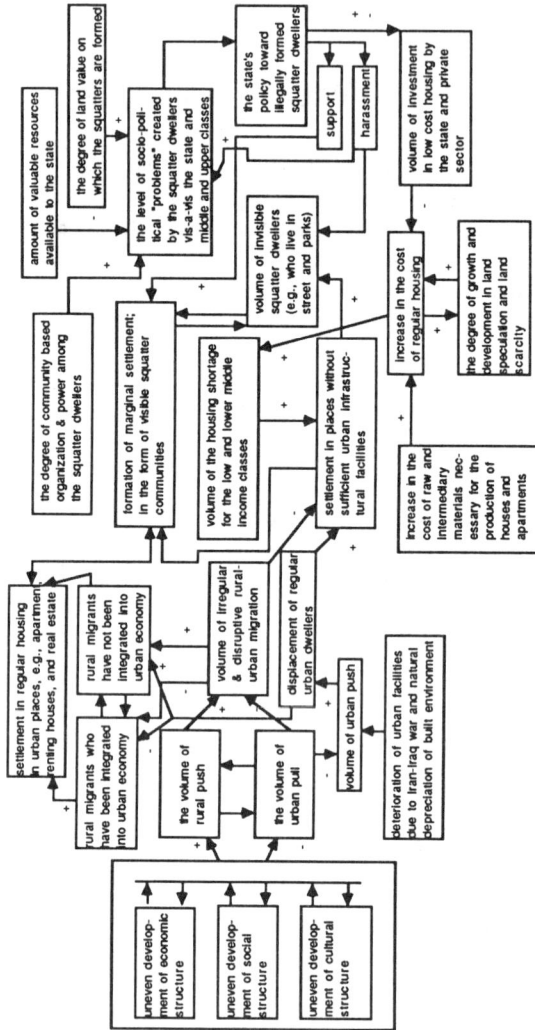

In conclusion, housing shortage in general and squatter settlement formation, in its diverse types, as a response to such a crisis in particular, are partly the structural outcomes of rapid and irregular rural-urban migration. The pattern of squatter settlement in relation to migration, housing crisis, the state, and other historically pertinent variables is schematically expressed in diagram 8.1.

The author believes that as long as the tide of unemployed, landless, and culturally deprived rural migrants is not effectively incorporated into the productive and dynamic sectors of the rural/urban economy, and as long as the housing industries are monopolistically controlled by private enterprises, more squatter settlements and more housing shortages will be the dominant features of the main urban centers of Iranian societies in the future. In the next chapter, the conclusion, a more comprehensive solution to the problem of irregular rural-urban migration and squatter settlements will be offered.

CHAPTER IX

CONCLUSION & POLICY
RECOMMENDATIONS

This book has analyzed the broad socio-economic causes and consequences of irregular and disrupting rural-urban migration in the developing countries, with special attention to Iran. Although there are significant differences among the developing countries, it was emphasized that the experiences and problems of urbanization and industrialization in Iran and other developing countries are far more similar to one another than they are to the European experiences of urbanization and industrialization in the 18th and 19th centuries.

The major problems of industrialization such as rapid population growth, formation of a super industrial reserve army, unbalanced urbanization and population concentrations, housing crises, irregular migration, political repression and crises in the state's legitimacy, economic instability and the subordinate position of the state in the world system are often simultaneously present in the majority of developing countries. More specifically, the Iranian case study showed that these variables not only exist but also tend to reinforce each other at various levels of society. In other words, a comprehensive explanation of irregular rural-urban migration should embrace not only economic variables but also social, demographic, cultural, and political variables as well. These autonomous and yet interpenetrating structures determine either directly the volume and pattern of migration or indirectly through the interaction effects that they impose upon each other. Thus, it is rather the mutual penetration of these structures that set the social milieu for the emergence of irregular and disrupting rural exodus.

It was found that the overall functioning of these interpenetrating structures removed the the rural population from the countryside, and at the same time repelled the rural migrants and other urban dwellers from being integrated into the socio-economic institutions of the cities. Thus, the crisis of rural exodus does not lie in the question of why people leave the countryside, but rather why the migrants cannot be absorbed and institutionalized by the major urban centers. Why does the rural resident leave the countryside when there is no opportunity for integration in the cities?

To answer these paradoxical questions it is suggested that the processes of irregular migration must be seen and analyzed from both "rural" and "urban" points of view. It is important to determine, first, the socio-economic and politico-cultural factors that expel and uproot the village dwellers and distort their communal social structure and, second, how these interpenetrating structures prevent the migrants and uprooted village dwellers from being absorbed and institutionalized in the socio-economic fabrics of the cities.

The study suggests that irregular and disrupting migration is formed only when there is a high level of rural push and a low level of rural pull in the country. In respect to these two broad conditions, the author strived to answer the following questions in order to identify the major concrete variables of irregular migration:

(1) What dimensions are rural push made of?

(2) What are the factors of rural push in each dimension?

(3) What are the dimensions and factors of urban pull in the city?

(4) Why are these factors unable to provide the favorable socio-economic conditions to integrate and institutionalize the migrants?

In an empirical study of industrialization and urbanization in Iran, the following key relations were discovered as the explanation of the massive irregular rural-urban migration:

A. There has been an acute disjunction between rural and urban centers at economic, social, cultural levels.

B. Migration is primarily triggered as a function of the level of disparity in the spatial distribution of valuable resources such as economic opportunities, cultural gratification, and symbolic status. While there might be no substantial employment opportunities for the rural migrants per se, the volume of irregular migration is determined by the combined structural effects of economic, social, and cultural variables as they distort the socio-economic structure of both places of origin and destination.

C. The distortion of the socio-economic structure of rural places predominantly occurs at economic levels and it involves the disarticulation of communal production relations and land relations. It was observed that rapid population growth coupled with the breakdown of local cultural systems on many occasions have complemented the overall distortion of economic relations of production, specifically at the level of land relations in the countryside (e.g., land concentration and landlessness, decline in productivity).

D. Similarly, in the major urban centers where the rural migrants choose to move, the combined effects of economic, social, and cultural variables have been to prevent the urban economy to grow in

151

accordance to the need of the migrants and the independent national economy (e.g., capital intensive technology, housing shortage, cultural superiority of the cities). The specific results of such structural effects have been the stagnation of the manufacturing sector at the stage of industrial take-off. It was concluded that the volume of irregular rural-urban migration tends to increase as the disparity increases between rural push and urban pull. Specifically in the case of Iran, the capacity of the urban economy was so limited that not only was the great proportion of rural migrants marginalized but also many urban dwellers were expelled to marginal economic and social conditions.

E. The role of the state in promoting the aforementioned conditions of disrupting migration has been very critical in the Iranian case and it is fruitful to summarize its basis and properties in the context of migration.

First, the state was highly dependent on the core capitalist nations. In the majority of cases, policies formulated for capitalist development and industrialization in Iran were predominantly formed by the foreign advisers and large multinational corporations. Such influences on the content of policy recommendation often generated improper choices of technology (e.g., heavy reliance on labor saving technology, excessive use of tractors on arid lands without promoting irrigation systems) and maldistribution of resources in space (e.g., heavy investment in Tehran city and in other major urban centers while ignoring the rural sectors and agricultural economy).

Second, since the state was heavily dependent on other core nations, it did not pay adequate attention to the role of popular mass participation in various national programs. For example, the land reform was drafted and operationalized by the top Iranian bureaucrats and the American advisers who did not deeply appreciate the constructive role of grass-root organization and popular participation in program-implementation. In most instances, the masterminds of reform were either alien to social arrangements in Iranian villages or themselves belonged to the landed oligarchy. In fact the *growing landlessness after the implementation of reform* should be understood in that context.

The chance of success in a government-run program increases as more underprivileged social groups are incorporated into all stages of the program. Mass involvement in the implementation of programs acts as a potent resistor to the participation of self-interested bureaucrats who often serve their own idiosyncratic interests and privileges.

Recognizing the importance and significance of popular participation in a successful implementation of reform in the Third World, the author will proceed and make the following concrete recommendations for the problem of migration in Iran. Given the multidimensional nature and causes of irregular migration, the recommendations will be provided

152

for each dimension separately in the following section.

Migration and Policy Recommendations

Rural migration, regardless of its volume or intensity, is often a contributory positive factor to socio-economic development under the following conditions: (1) high rural push and high urban pull; (2) low urban pull and low rural push; and (3) low rural push and high urban pull (see Diagram 9.1). To change the pattern of irregular rural-urban migration to a regular one, the proposed model of migration suggests that the state should concentrate its resources at economic, social, and cultural levels in rural areas and adopt Type (2). Urban regions are already highly unbalanced and overconcentrated, and it is almost impossible to find the long-term strategical solution in the urban areas, namely in Type (1). To reach such a goal in rural areas, the following policies should be implemented to reduce the rural push in the countryside.

Economic Level

At this level, the ultimate goal is to increase employment opportunities and to reduce income inequality in the rural areas. To do so the state with the help, cooperation, and mass participation of underprivileged groups (e.g., small land holders, landless khushnesheen, unemployed rural migrants in the cities) should implement the following programs:

1. Modernization and reconstruction of small scale household industries in the villages.

2. Heavy investment in non-farm industries which are directly and indirectly interconnected to the agricultural economy. These industries, while improving the agricultural economy, can also reduce the unemployment rate created by the slowing down of agricultural activities in cold seasons.

3. It has been found that too much parcelization of land brings down the level of productivity and thus income. It is important, given the specificity of the Iranian agricultural economy, to collectivize farm lands into units larger than 20 hectares. Twenty hectares of land is considered the smallest land unit in which a tractor, fertilizers, an irrigation

153

Diagram 9.1

Typology of Migration Based on Push-Pull Socio-economic Variables

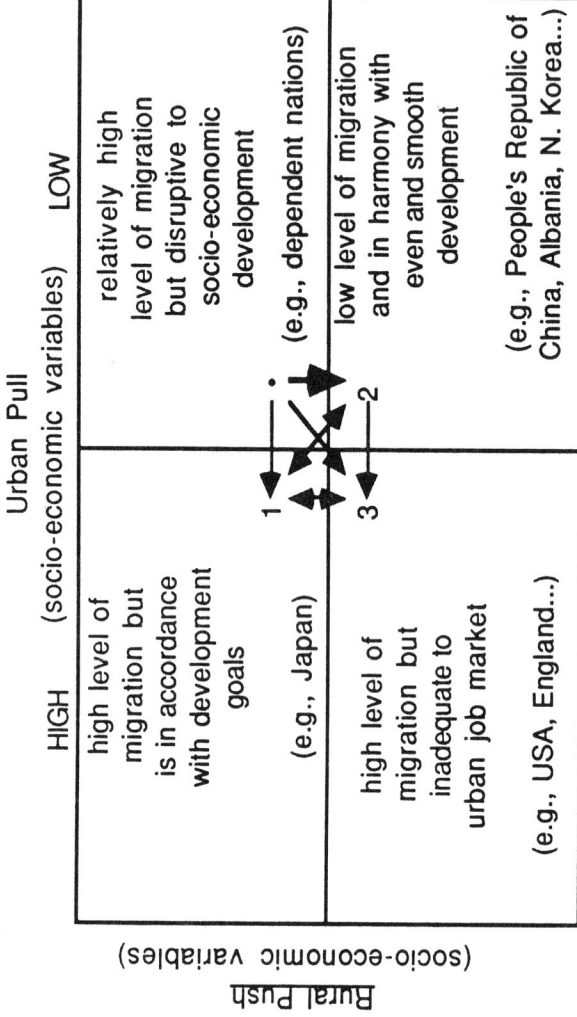

	Urban Pull	
	HIGH (socio-economic variables)	LOW
HIGH (socio-economic variables)	high level of migration but is in accordance with development goals (e.g., Japan)	relatively high level of migration but disruptive to socio-economic development (e.g., dependent nations)
LOW	high level of migration but inadequate to urban job market (e.g., USA, England...)	low level of migration and in harmony with even and smooth development (e.g., People's Republic of China, Albania, N. Korea...)

Rural Push (socio-economic variables)

system, and pesticides can be widely and effectively utilized.

4. Extension of farming lands by improving the nation-wide irrigation system and *radical* land redistribution among the landless peasants and unemployed urban dwellers who are familiar with agricultural activities.

5. Diversification of the occupational structure in villages by discouraging monoculturalization of the agrarian economy.

6. Equal distribution of credits and the state's sponsored funds among small and landless peasants. Again, peasants must have their own selected representatives and they should be given power in formulating the content of the credit system designed for the agrarian economy.

7. Protecting the peasants from unwarranted bankruptcy by introducing insurance system to village workers and farmers.

8. Heavy emphasis on the use of capital-saving technology while encouraging farmers to increase their productivity for higher income. This can be achieved by relying on fertilizers, hybrid seeds, and adequate watering.

Demographic Level

Population growth in and of itself is a double-edged sword which simultaneously increases the volume of rural push and decreases the volume of urban pull, the conditions that lead to the acceleration of irregular rural-urban migration. It is known that programs for population control in most of the developing countries, including Iran, have been predominantly unsuccessful.

Demographic variables are extensively shaped and influenced by economic and cultural variables. Significant reduction in economic uncertainty at the level of *household* in rural areas would have a significant effect on population control. Similarly, traditional value system and religious upbringing at the cultural level are important elements in fertility behavior. It is, thus, recommended that any program that deals with population variables, specifically fertility behavior, should incorporate the opinions and advice of religious authorities in writing, drafting, and implementing a population program.

Social Level

At this level, the general goal is to redistribute the social services more evenly in space. So far, the trend has been toward overconcentration of necessary services in the large urban centers. This trend must be reversed in order to increase the level of rural pull in the Iranian villages. To reach such a goal the following programs are suggested:

1. Construction of roads to remote villages in order to facilitate the smooth flow of social services.

2. Creation of small scale educational centers which can familiarize the farmers with the modern technology of farming and farming related industries.

3. Training some of the local residents in basic health related skills. The experience of bare-foot-doctors in China in formulating such programs has proven to be very useful.

4. Providing scholarship for those students who would like to major in health related subjects and are willing to work in rural areas for five or more years.

5. Eliminating the parasitical urban middleman (e.g., "Salaf Khar" in Iran's traditional Bazaar) from the distribution of farm products and instead creating cooperative organizations for the storage and distribution of the products. These cooperatives should be set up by the farmers themselves and they should be able to distribute the farm goods directly from the direct producers to the immediate consumers. By the elimination of middleman distributors it is likely that the real income and solidarity among farmers would increase which would directly benefit the village community as a whole.

Cultural Level

Cultural programs that are designed to enhance the pulling capacity of rural areas should ideally strive for a radical re-organization of the existing distorted culture towards collectivism, national pride, identity, and creativity. That is to say, cultural programs should broadly endeavour to create new and decolonized humans, who can think, create, and act as a collective entity which represents not only his/her own interests but also those who are not present and cannot defend their own interests.

It is out of the scope of this study to make policy recommendations for cultural changes. It is the major task of religious leaders, political activists, and revolutionaries to create a new and practical agenda for advancement of humanism and the actualization of vast human potentialities. To create a conscious, productive, and passionate human in the contemporary world of capitalism requires the necessary social, political, historical, and economic conditions that are about to come. Our participation and intervention will tremendously accelerate this process.

BIBLIOGRAPHY

Abrams, Charles. *Man's Struggle for Shelter in an Urbanizing World.* Cambridge: MIT Press, 1964.

Adams, Richard. "Harnessing Technological Development." *In Rethinking Modernization: Anthropological Perspectives.* Edited by John J. Poggie, Jr., Robert Lynch. Westport, Connecticut: Greenwood Press, 1974.

Alizadeh, Mohammad & Kazeroonee, Kazem. *Migration and Urbanization in Iran.* Tehran, Iran. Plan and Budget Organization, in Persian, 1984.

Amjad. Mohammad. "The Origin of Iranian Revolution." *Ph.D. dissertation, University of California, Riverside.* Department of Political Science, 1985.

Ashraf, Ahmad. "Iran: Imperialism, Class and Modernization from Above." *Ph.D. dissertation, New School for Social Research,* 1971.

Ashraf, Ahmad and et al. "The Role of the Rural Organization in Rural Development: the Case of Iran." *Tehran, Iran. Plan and Budget Organization,* 1977.

Bahr, Howard M. *Skid Row: An Introduction to Disaffiliation.* Oxford University Press, 1973.

Bank Markazi Iran. Anual Reports. Tehran, Iran, 1971-1982.

------------------. *A Survey of Problems and difficulties in Iran's Industries.* The Department of Economic Statistics, in Persian, 1980.

Barraclough, S. *Notas Sobre Tenencia de la Tierra en American Latina.* Santiago de Chile: ICIRA (1968).

Berry, Brian. "City Size Distribution and Economic Development." *Economic Development and Cultural Change,* no. 9 (1961).

Bharier, Julian. *Economic Development in Iran: 1900-1972.* New York: Oxford University press, 1971.

----------. "The Growth of Towns and Villages in Iran, 1900-1966." *Middle Eastern Studies*, no. 8, (January 1972).

Braverman, Harry. *Labor and Monopoly Capital: The Degradation of Work in the Twentieth Century.* Monthly Review Press, 1974.

Cardoso, F. H. "Industrialization, Occupational Structure, and Social Stratification in Latin America." *In Constructive Change in Latin America. Edited by Cole Balsier.* University of Pittsburg Press, (1968).

Castells, Manuel. *The Urban Question.* The MIT Press, 1979.

----------. Urban Social Movements and the Struggle for Democracy: the Citizens' Movement in Madrid. *International Journal of Urban & Regional Research*, 1978.

Chase-Dunn, Christopher. "The Effects if International Economic Dependence on Development and Inequality: A Cross-National Study." *American Sociological Review*, no. 40 (December 1980).

Danesh, Abol Hassan. *An Introduction to a Theory of Irregular Rural-urban Migration in Developing Countries.* Tehran. Iran: Plan and Budget Organization, Department of Population and Manpower, in Persian (1984).

----------. *The Causes of the Expansion of Unproductive Jobs in the Metropolitan Cities of Developing Countries.* Tehran, Iran: Plan and Budget Organization, in Persian, 1984.

Davis, Kingsley. "Urbanization and Development of Pre-industrial Areas." *Economic Development and Cultural Change* III(October 1965).

Etemad Moghadam, Fatemeh. "The Effect of Farm Size and Management System on Agricultural Production." *Ph.D. dissertation, Oxford University.*

Fernandez, Raul. *The Us-Mexico Border Economy.* Monthly Review Press, 1977.

Fischoff, Ephraimi. The Protestant Ethic and the Spirit of Capitalism: "The History of a Controversy." *Social Research,* XI, 1944.

Frank, Andrew. "Urban Poverty in Latin America." *Studies in Comparative International Development,* vol. 4, no. 11 (1966).

Furtado, Celso. *Development and underdevelopment.* University of California, Berkeley Press, 1964.

Gheiyasee, Mojeydean. *Amalkard Bakhshe Behdasht va Darman Teyye Barnamehaye Omranee Gozashteh va Tasveere Moojood.* Tehran, Iran. Plan and Budget Organization, in Persian, 1982.

Giddens, Anthony. *Capitalism and Modern Social Theory.* Cambridge University Press, 1971.

Goblot, Henri. "Dans E'ancien Iran, Les Techniques de L' eau et La Grand Histoire." *Annual ESC* (May-June 1963).

Gottdiener, Mark. "Hegemony and Mass Culture: A Semitic Approach." *American Journal of Sociology,* vol. 90, no. 5 (1985).

----------------. *The Social Production of Urban Space.* Texas University Press, 1985.

Griffin, Heith. *Land Concentration and Rural Poverty.* Cox and Wyman LTD., 1976.

Guess, George M. "pasture Expansion, Forestry, and Development Contradiction: The Case of Costa Rica." *Studies in Comparative International Development,* no. XIV (Spring 1979).

Halliday, Fred. *Iran: Dictatorship and Development.* New York: Penguin, 1979.

Hemmasi, M. *Barasee Angeezehayeh va Peyamadhaee Moohajerathayeh Roosta Nesheenan be Shahr dar Ostan Fars.* Shiraz university, Iran, 1979.

----------------. "Tehran in Transition: A Study in Comparative Factorial Ecology," in *The Population of Iran: A Selection of Readings,* ed. Jamshid Momeni, *East-West Population Institutes, 1977.*

160

Hirshman, Alberto. *The Strategy of Economic Development.* Yale University Press, 1958.

Hooglund, Eric. "The Khwushnishin Population of Iran." *Iranian Studies,* no.6(1973).

------------. *Land and Revolution in Iran, 1960-1980.* University Press of Texas, 1982.

Housain Zadeh Daleer, K. *The Tabriz Shanty Dwellers.* Tabriz University Press(in Persian), 1982.

ILO. *Employment, Income, Social Protections, New Information Technology,* 1984.

Karush, G. E. "Plantation, Population, and Poverty: The Roots of Demographic Crisis in El Salvador. "*Studies in Comparative International Development,* no. 13, (1979).

Katozian, M. A. "Land Reform in Iran: A Case Study in the Political Economy of Social Engineering." *Journal of Peasant Studies,* vol. 1, no. 2 (1974).

--------------. "Oil Versus Agriculture: A Case of Dual Resource Depletion in Iran." *Journal of Peasant Studies,* no. 5, pp. 347-369, August(1975).

Kazemi, Farhad. *Revolution and Poverty in Iran.* New York University Press, 1980.

Keddie, N. "The Iranian Village Before and After Land Reform." *Journal of Contemporary History,* no. 3 (1968).

Khaza-ee, Ahmad. *The Peculiarities of Manufacturing Employment in Iran: 1966-1976.* Tehran, Iran. Plan and Budget Organization (in Persian), 1984.

Khamesi, Farhad. "Land Reform in Iran." *Monthly Review,* no. 21(1969).

Khorasanezadeh, Ali. "Barrasee Eghtasadi va Ejtema-ee Goudnesheenun Jounoobe Tehran." *B.A. Thesis, Dr. Sha-ree-attee University,*

Tehran, Iran, 1980.

Khusravi, K. *Pazhuhishi dar Jamehe Roostaee Iran.* Tehran, Iran: Payman Publisher, 1979.

Klark, Jane & Carey, Andrew. "Iranian Agriculture and Its Development: 1952-1973." *International Journal of Middle East Studies,* Vol. 3, no. 1 (1966).

Kolko, Gabriel. "Max Weber on America: Theory and Evidence," *in Studies in Philosophy of History, ed. by George H. Nadel,* New York: Harper and Row, 1965.

Lambton, Ann S. *The Persian Land Reform: 1962-1966.* London: Oxford University Press, 1969.

Lee, E. S. "A Theory of Migration." *Demography,* vol. 3, no. 1 (1966).

Lewis. W. A. "Economic Development with Unlimited Supplies of Labor." *The Manchester School of Economic and Social Studies,* no. 22, May (1954).

Lloyd, Peter. *Shantytowns of Third World: Slums of Hope?* Pelican Book, 1979.

Lominitz, L. *Network and Marginality: Life in Mexican Shantytown.* Academic Press, 1977.

Lowe, Stuart. *Urban Social Movements: The City after Castells.* St. Martin's Press, New York, 1986.

Magdoff, H. "The American Empire and the U.S. Economy." *In Robert Rhodes, Imperialism and Underdevelopment.* Monthly Review Press, 1970.

Majeedee, Abdol Majeed. *Dor Na-ma-yee Egh-te-sa-dee Va Ejtema-ee Iran.* Plan and Budget Organization, 1975.

McClelland, David C. "The Achievement Motive in Economic Growth." *In Hoselitz and Moore, Industrialization and Society,* 1963.

Mangin, William. "Latin American Squatter Settlements: A Problem and a Solution." *Latin American Research Review* 2(3) (1967).

Marx, Karl. *Selected Works.* Moscow: Progress Publishers; London: Laurence & Wishart, 1969.

Mashhoodee, Sohrab. *Barnameh Ta-mean Maskan va Bahre-varee as Raveshe Ertegha Marhaleh-be-Marhaleh Sat-he Sokoonat.* Tehran, Iran. Plan and Budget Organization, 1980.

Ministry of Agriculture in Iran. *Sar Shoomaree Keshavarzee Sal-le 1339.* Published by Plan and Budget Organization, 1970.

-----------------------. *Sar Shoomaree Keshavarzee Sal-le 1353.* Published by Plan and Budget Organization, 1975.

Ministry of Health. *Daftar Omoore Jam-eyat va Bar Rasee-hi-ye Amaree va Barnameh Reezee* Mashinee. 1971.

Ministry of Housing in Iran. *Vezarat-te Maskan va Shahr Sazee.* Various issues, 1960-1980.

Ministry of Labor in Iran. *Natayeje Tarhe Amarre va Bar Rasee Masa-el Kolle Neeyroye Ensanee va Eshteghal Manateghe Shahree* 1983.

Montgomery, John D. *International Dimensions of Land Reform.* Westview Press, 1984.

Morse, Richard. "Latin American Cities: Aspects of Function and Structure." *Comparative Studies in Society and History, no. 4 (July 1962).*

Myrdal, Goundar. *Asian Drama: An Inquiry into the Poverty of Nations.* Pantheon, a division of Random House, 1968.

Nelson, Joan. "The Urban Poor: The Disruption or Political Integration?" *World Politics,* (April 1970).

Paige, Jeffery. *Agrarian Revolution: Social Movements and Export Agriculture in the Underdeveloped World.* New York, Free Press, 1975.

Pickvance, C. G. *The State and Collective Consumption.* Unit 24 of Open University course D202 Urban Change and Conflict, Milton Keynes: The Open University Press, 1982.

Perlman, Janice E. *The Myth of Marginality: Urban Poverty and Politics in Rio de Janeiro.* University Press, 1976.

Plan & Budget Organization of Iran. *Barnameh Omranee Panjoum Keshvar.* Tehran, Iran, 1976.

Plan & Budget Organization of Iran. *Indicators of Income Distribution in Iran.* Tehran, Iran(in Persian), 1983.

Plan & Budget Organization of Iran. *Economic Trends of Iran.* Tehran, Iran, 1978.

Plan & Budget Organization of Iran. *Nakhosteen Santeze Etelaat Moojood: Shenasaeey Manateghee Gerehee- Bohranee ya Mosaed,* 1975.

Plan & Budget Organization of Iran. *Iranian National Census* 1956, 1966, 1976.

Plan & Budget Organization of Iran. *Iran: Economic Survey of Greater Iran.* Tehran, Iran, 1966. Statistical Center of Iran. Agricultural Census, 1960, 1974.

Portes, A. "Modernity and Development: A Critique." *Studies in Comparative International Development,* no. 8, pp. 249-79, Fall (1973).

Quarterly Economic Review of Iran. *Annual Supplement,* **1978.**

Rafe-ye, Hommayoon. *Bar-rasee E-lal va Avame-lle Moohajert-e Roosta-ey-yan dar Ostan Hammadan.* Tehran, Iran. Plan and Budget Organization, 1974.

Ranis, G. and Fei, J. "A Theory of Economic Development." *American Economic Review,* vol. 51, no. 4(September), 1961.

Ravenstein, E. "The Laws of Migration." *Journal of the Royal Statistical Society* no. 52 (June), 1889.

Redfield, Robert. "The Folk Society." In *Classic Essays in the Culture of Cities. Edited by Richard Sennett.* New York: Appleton, Century, Crofts, 1968.

Research Group. "A Survey of the Rural Cooperatives in Province of Hammadan." *Quarterly Journal of Economic Research,* vol. 7, no. 17 (1970).

Reza, Ali M. "What Happened to Iran's Oil Revenues?" *Iran Voice,* no. 14, January, (1980).

Samuelsson, Kurt. *Religion and Economic Action.* Translated by E. Geoffrey French (Stockholm: Scandinavian University Books, 1957), 1961.

Scoville, James G. "The Labor Market and Revolution in Iran." A working paper, 1984.

Shaw, Paul R. "land Tenure and Rural Exodus in Latin America." *Economic Development and Cultural Change,* no. 23, October, (1974).

Sjaastad, L. "The Cost and Return of Human Migration." *Journal of Political Science,* part 2 (October), 1962.

Sohrabee, Hamid & et al. *The Pattern of Income Distribution in Rural and Urban Regions in Iran.* Plan & Budget Organization, in Persian, 1981.

Soofi, Abdollah Siavash. "Iranian Fiscal Policy, Foreign Trade, and Economic Development: 1930-1978." *Ph.D. dissertation, University of California, Riverside,* 1980.

Sovani, N. V. "The Analysis of Over-Urbanization." *Economic Development and Cultural Change,* vol. 12, no.2, (1964).

Spengler, O. *The Decline of the West.* London: Allen and Unwin, 1928.

Statistical Center of Iran. *National Census (Sarshomaree Omomee Nofoos va Maskan),* 1956, 1966, 1976.

Statistical Center of Iran. *Amar Kargha-ne-hi-ey Boozorge San-at-ee Iran. Tehran, Iran, 1966.*

Statistical Center of Iran. *Amar Kargha-ne-hi-ey Boozorge San-at-ee Iran. Tehran, Iran, 1974.*

Statistical Center of Iran. *Nataye-je Amarge-ree Nee-royee Ensanee Shahr-e Tehran.* Tehran, Iran, 1972.

Statistical Center of Iran. *Nataye-je Amarge-ree Nee-royee Ensanee Ko-lle Keshvar.* Tehran, Iran, 1973.

Statistical Center of Iran. *The Second Stage of Agricultural Census.* Tehran, Iran, 1974.

Statistical Center of Iran. *Nata-ye-je Amarge-ree as Bood-jeh Khanvarhayee Roosta-ee.* Tehran, Iran, 1980.

Strokes, Charles. "A Theory of Slums." *Land Economics,* no. 38, August, (1962).

Todaro, M.P. *Economic Development in the Third World.* Free Press, 1980.

------------ "A Model of Labor Migration and Urban Unemployment in Less Developed Countries." *American Economic Review,* vol. 59, no. 1 (1969).

Theodorson, G. A. *Modern Dictionary of Sociology.* Thomas Y. Crowell Company, 1970.

Tucker, R. C. *The Marx-Engels Reader.* New York: Norton, 1972.

Turner, John C. "Uncontrolled Urban Settlements: Problems and Policies." In *The Cities in Newly Developing Countries: Reading on Urbanism and Urbanization. Edited by Gerald Breese.* Englewood Cliffs, New Jersey: Prentice-Hall, 1969.

United Nations. *FAO Production Year Book.* Food and Agricultural Organization, 1972.

United Nations. "Migration, Population Growth, and Development." *Population Report,* vol. 11, no. 4(1983).

United Nations. "Pattern of Urban and Rural Population Growth." *Department of International Economic and Social Affairs: Population Studies,* no. 68, New York (1980).

United Nations. *Quarterly Bulletin of Statistics for Asia and the Pacific,* vol. XI, no. 2, June, (1981).

US Census of Population. *1960 Number of Inhabitants,* United States, summary. Final report, P.C. (1) 1A (1961).

Wirth, Louis. "Urbanism as a Way of Life." *American Journal of Sociology,* no. 44 (1938).

Zendehdel, Hassan. *The Structure of Labor Force in the Agricultural Sector of Iran.* Plan and Budget Organization, the Division of Population and Manpower, in Persian, 1983.

Zeitlin Irving M. *Ideology and the Development of Sociological Theory.* Prentice-Hall INC., 1968.

Zonis, Marvin. *The Political Elite of Iran.* Princeton: Princeton University Press, 1971.

** About the Author **

Abol Hassan Danesh was born in Ghazvin city of Iran in May 14, 1952. He earned his B.A. in accounting from Tehran University in 1974. He continued his education in the field of sociology in the U.S. He earned his M.A. in sociology from California State University at L.A. in 1979 and his Ph.D. degree from the University of California at Riverside in 1985. He is currently teaching as assistant professor of sociology at Colby College.

In Persian language, Dr. Danesh has also published books and articles on various issues of underdevelopment in Third World, prticularly on the subject of migration, homelessness, and informal jobs. He has one year old daughter with the name of Shabnam.